Chinese History and Folktales

An Enthralling Journey Through Ancient Dynasties, Cultural Legends, and Timeless Stories from China

© **Copyright 2025 - All rights reserved.**

The content contained within this book may not be reproduced, duplicated, or transmitted without direct written permission from the author or the publisher.

Under no circumstances will any blame or legal responsibility be held against the publisher, or author, for any damages, reparation, or monetary loss due to the information contained within this book, either directly or indirectly.

Legal Notice:

This book is copyright protected. It is only for personal use. You cannot amend, distribute, sell, use, quote, or paraphrase any part, or the content within this book, without the consent of the author or publisher.

Disclaimer Notice:

Please note the information contained within this document is for educational and entertainment purposes only. All effort has been executed to present accurate, up-to-date, reliable, and complete information. No warranties of any kind are declared or implied. Readers acknowledge that the author is not engaging in the rendering of legal, financial, medical, or professional advice. The content within this book has been derived from various sources. Please consult a licensed professional before attempting any techniques outlined in this book.

By reading this document, the reader agrees that under no circumstances is the author responsible for any losses, direct or indirect, that are incurred as a result of the use of the information contained within this document, including, but not limited to, errors, omissions, or inaccuracies.

Free limited time bonus

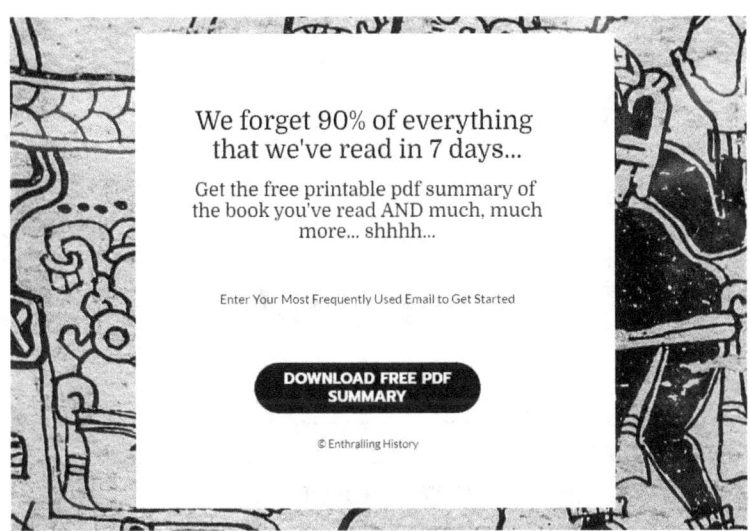

Stop for a moment. We have a free bonus set up for you. The problem is this: we forget 90% of everything that we read after 7 days. Crazy fact, right? Here's the solution: we've created a printable, 1-page pdf summary for this book that you're reading now. All you have to do to get your free pdf summary is to go to the following website:
https://livetolearn.lpages.co/enthrallinghistory/

Or, Scan the QR code!

Once you do, it will be intuitive. Enjoy, and thank you!

Table of Contents

PART 1: HISTORY OF CHINA 1
   INTRODUCTION 3
   CHAPTER 1: THE PREHISTORY OF CHINA 5
   CHAPTER 2: DAWN OF THE DYNASTIES 9
   CHAPTER 3: SILK AND THE SWORD 18
   CHAPTER 4: FROM THE TANG TO THE SONG 26
   CHAPTER 5: THE MAJESTY OF THE MING DYNASTY 37
   CHAPTER 6: THE QING— CHINA'S LAST DYNASTY 45
   CHAPTER 7: WORLD WAR II AND CHINA'S CIVIL WAR 63
   CHAPTER 8: RED CHINA RISING 69
   CHAPTER 9: A STRANGE MIX OF REPRESSION AND REFORM 78
   CHAPTER 10: CHINA DURING THE 21ST CENTURY 85
   CONCLUSION: CHINA–AN EXERCISE IN STRATEGIC PATIENCE 93
PART 2: CHINESE FOLKTALES AND LEGENDS 95
   HOW TO PRONOUNCE PINYIN 97
   INTRODUCTION 98
   CHAPTER 1: CHINA'S FOLKLORIC FOUNDATIONS 100
   CHAPTER 2: THE JADE EMPEROR'S REALM 108
   CHAPTER 3: LEGENDS FROM THE SILK ROAD 118
   CHAPTER 4: TALES OF THE LOTUS POND 128
   CHAPTER 5: THE GIFT OF THE DRAGON 138
   CHAPTER 6: BAMBOO AND ITS SIGNIFICANCE 149
   CHAPTER 7: PHOENIX LEGENDS 158

CHAPTER 8: WARRIORS OF DESTINY 166
CHAPTER 9: MOUNTAINS AND RIVERS: MAGICAL LANDSCAPES 174
CHAPTER 10: MAGICAL LANTERNS AND CHINESE FESTIVALS 183
CONCLUSION 191
HERE'S ANOTHER BOOK BY ENTHRALLING HISTORY THAT YOU MIGHT LIKE 193
FREE LIMITED TIME BONUS 194
FURTHER READING AND REFERENCE 195
IMAGE SOURCES 198

Part 1: History of China

An Enthralling Journey Through Ancient Dynasties, Cultural Splendor, Revolution, and Modernization

Introduction

China has a long and fascinating history. This is perhaps an understatement, considering the fact that China has been part of history since practically the beginning of the written record. As much as China is a big part of our lives today (just think of the wide range of products from Amazon or retail stores that more than likely carry the tag "Made in China"), China was also a big part of the ancient world.

The ancient Greeks knew about China, as did the Romans. China's famed Silk Road cut a path across the continent, stretching from Asia all the way to the heart of the Roman Empire. These crossroads between East and West brought not just exotic goods but also diverse cultures, innovative ideas, and even religious and philosophical expressions. The religious teachings of Buddhism and the philosophical musings of Confucianism were allowed to travel far and wide due to the routes along the Silk Road.

Westerners speak of the Golden Rule of treating others as one would like to be treated, but Confucianism has the Silver Rule, which speaks of not imposing oneself on others, just as one would not wish to be imposed upon. Even if far-flung nations did not become Confucian, it is likely that the core teachings and values of Eastern religious and philosophical systems left a lasting impression on those who heard of them.

For a long time, China seemed to be a far-off marvel. It was known to be a great and majestic civilization, but it was seemingly cut off from the rest of the world. Nevertheless, it was still at the heart of all that was valuable and worthwhile. Traders and explorers such as Marco Polo would risk life and limb just to see it with their own eyes. Outside forces gazed greedily at the riches that China had to offer, wishing to seize them for their own. It was for precisely this reason that China erected thick and sturdy walls to protect itself from the threat of incursions.

These walls could not keep everyone out, though. China would be periodically infringed upon by the Mongols, Manchus, Japanese, and Europeans. Even so, China's robust culture always proved too well entrenched for any outside force to dominate. The best they could do was temporarily oversee China's massive civilization; there was no way that they could fully control it forever. After all, China has blazed its own unique and vital path through history and will likely continue to do so for the foreseeable future.

Chapter 1: The Prehistory of China

"Death and life have their determined appointments; riches and honors depend upon heaven."

   -*Confucius*[i]

   According to tradition, China's origins date back some five thousand years; needless to say, China has a rather in-depth history, to say the least. The Chinese civilization is one of the oldest continuous civilizations on the planet. Of course, the Chinese civilization has undergone some rather incredible transformations over the millennia. Even so, there is a core group of shared ideals that has remained among the Chinese to this very day. Chinese principles regarding war, work ethic, and family life, which date back to the likes of Chinese philosophers such as Confucius, have had a strong line of continuity.

   When it came to war, the Chinese believed that brains were better than brawn. Rather than rushing into battle, they preferred to outthink their enemies and figure out how to win without even fighting, if possible. That idea goes all the way back to Sun Tzu, a Chinese general and military strategist who basically said that the best kind of victory is the one you don't even have to fight for. As for work ethic, the Chinese put a huge emphasis on hard work and doing your part. Thanks to thinkers like Confucius, there was a strong sense that everyone had a role to play—whether in the family or in society—and that meant showing up, working hard, and keeping things running smoothly.

---

[i] Brewer, D. *Quotes of Confucius and Their Interpretations: A Words of Wisdom Collection Book*. 2020. Pg. 42.

While the actual founding of China is shrouded in mystery, it is believed to date back thousands of years. Human habitation of the region goes back much further than that, at least a million years ago. This was long before recorded history and long before human civilization was even a conscious thought.

These early humans were not *Homo sapiens*, like we are today, but rather an earlier branch of humanity known as *Homo erectus*. These early humans lived in the region we now call China during the Paleolithic period. They left artifacts all across the region until they eventually disappeared from the fossil record. The exact nature of their disappearance is still the subject of some debate. Some even argue that they might not have disappeared at all; they might have merged with the newly arriving *Homo sapiens*.

Homo sapiens first appeared in the fossil record of China around 100,000 years ago. Fossilized teeth were found inside Fuyan Cave, located in modern-day Dao County in China's Hunan province. Over thousands of years, people slowly began to spread out, adapting to their surroundings and developing new ways to survive. Over time, small groups of hunter-gatherers started figuring out how to make better tools, build simple shelters, and maybe even form the beginnings of spoken language. It was not exactly civilization yet, but they were laying the groundwork.

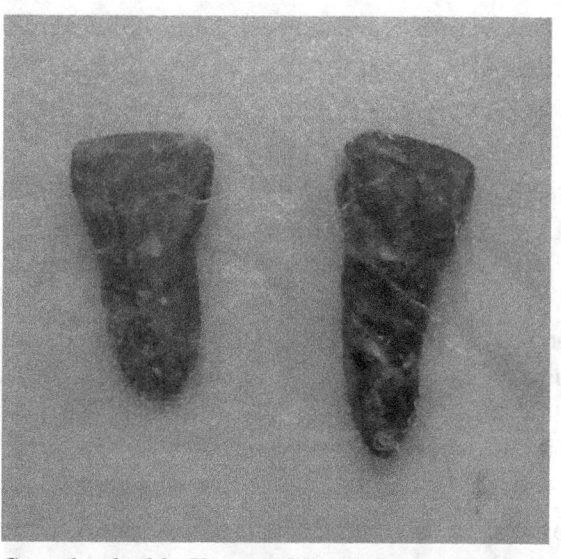

Casts of teeth of the Yuanmou Man, a subspecies of Homo erectus.[1]

During the Neolithic period, early humans first began to really band together, further building the foundation of what could be called a complex society. Instead of wandering around to forage and hunt, these early humans began to create early settlements. By doing so, they began to create the bonds of interconnectedness upon which civilization is built.

This was also the period in which widespread agriculture began to take shape. Agriculture is a key building block of any civilization. The one agricultural crop that came to dominate Chinese society was rice. Rice farms in China date back between eight thousand and nine thousand years ago. They were largely centered around China's Yangtze River. By 7000 BCE, humans lived up and down that river. By 5000 BCE, further habitation appeared along the nearby Huang He or, as it is often referred to, the Yellow River.

One group in particular, which archaeologists refer to as the Yangshao culture, took root in the Huang He Valley. This group expanded and became quite numerous. They lived near the Hung He and in the vicinity of another nearby waterway, the Wei River. The Yangshao were farmers who not only grew millet but also domesticated animals such as pigs and dogs.

Archaeologists first took note of the Yangshao culture because of their extensive pottery. They left traces of their complex pottery, which was made out of flint and jade, along the rivers where they worked and lived. They also forged complex burial sites. They dug earthen pit tombs, where they placed pottery and other important artifacts with their dearly departed. These actions seemed to indicate some early notion of an afterlife; it was as if the Yangshao were attempting to provide items that would be useful during their loved one's journey to the other side.

A pottery bottle from the Yangshao culture.[3]

Early prehistoric peoples, like the Yangshao culture, were the first to dream about the bigger things in life. They began to question who they were and where they came from. They questioned what it was that made them a unique, thinking individual, as well as what they desired from a larger society built on mutual interests. These early forays into the human condition and how it relates to the larger world would lead to the establishment of China's first major civilization.

Chapter 2: Dawn of the Dynasties

"It is better to light one small candle than to curse the darkness."
-Confucius[i]

Around 2070 BCE, the first Chinese dynasty—the Xia dynasty—was said to have emerged. For a long time, many scholars thought the Xia might have been more legend than fact. Later Chinese writers might have dreamed it up as a golden age, a shining example of what was lost when rulers got too comfortable on the throne. Like Atlantis, the Xia became a mix of memory and myth. It was part history, part cautionary tale.

But that story started to shift in the 20th century when a team of Chinese archaeologists uncovered the remains of what's now called the Erlitou culture. The site, located in Henan province, dates back to roughly the same time as the Xia dynasty is said to have existed. At first, the ruins were thought to belong to the later Shang dynasty. But over time, some researchers began linking Erlitou more closely with the Xia. Some even believe that the Erlitou site itself might have been one of the Xia capitals.

Still, not everyone agrees. Some scholars argue that the Erlitou culture had nothing to do with the Xia at all. Others go further back and trace its roots to the earlier Yangshao culture. The big challenge is that while Erlitou left behind clear archaeological remains, such as tools, pottery, weapons, and even some rather intricate bronze vessels, the Xia left no writing. Much of what we "know" about the Xia comes from texts written centuries later.

---

[i] Brewer, D. *Quotes of Confucius and Their Interpretations: A Words of Wisdom Collection Book.* Pg. 32.

A decorative plaque from the Erlitou culture.[5]

That's part of the mystery. Among the Erlitou artifacts are basic tools like arrowheads and fishhooks, the kind you might expect from a simpler society. But mixed in are finely crafted bronze tripod containers, which are thought to have been used in ceremonies. These signs of organization and craftsmanship suggest that Erlitou might have been more than just a cluster of villages. It might have been a state-level society, with rulers, rituals, and a system for getting things done.

So, while the Xia dynasty remains shrouded in legend, Erlitou is real. Whether Erlitou was the Xia, came after it, or had nothing to do with it at all is still up for debate. But just like the ruins of Troy, what was once dismissed as pure myth is starting to look a little more like history.

Most of the information about the Xia dynasty comes from ancient chroniclers. One such chronicler, a Chinese historian named Sima Qian, who lived from around 145 to 86 BCE, recorded some vague details on the subject. He spoke of a powerful leader named Huangdi, who is better known as the Yellow Emperor. Huangdi established a powerful civilization, which, according to Sima Qian, was the direct forerunner to the Xia dynasty. Huangdi was later succeeded by his grandson Zhuanxu, who was instrumental in laying the groundwork for the Xia dynasty.

Zhuanxu was the grandfather of the man who was traditionally ascribed as the founder of the Xia dynasty, Yu the Great. Yu is a fascinating, semi-mythical figure from China's past. One of the most interesting things about him and this time period was that he led China through a terrible natural disaster, which was described as a great flood. This flood story, like many others around the world, is uncannily similar to the famous biblical account of Noah's flood.

The fact that so many parts of the world have their own ancient account of a flood from around the same time period has led many to believe that a major deluge did indeed happen. Yu the Great was instrumental in leading his people through the crisis. In fact, it is said that he found ways to literally push back against or control the rising tide, which he did through supernatural means or by way of supernatural entities. However he did it, it is said that once the floods had been pushed back, Yu was able to rebuild his kingdom and make it even better than before.[i]

Several rulers are said to have followed this founding figure, with the last one being the tyrannical Jie, who is said to have lost the Mandate of Heaven, which gave him the right to rule, because of his corrupt and selfish behavior. According to ancient chroniclers, this was the reason why the Xia dynasty collapsed.

Modern scholars are cautious about accepting such claims at face value, though. There are, after all, quite a few examples in ancient times of one civilization conquering or overtaking another and then retroactively creating a mythologized account that condemns their predecessors while justifying their own usurpation. It is rare to find honest historical accounts in which a conquering nation or tribe actually states they wanted more territory to add to their power. It was (and still is) standard practice to make the conquered nation out to be the bad guy.

---

[i] Min, Anchee. *China: People, Place, Culture, History.* 2007. Pg. 237.

If you rewind ancient Chinese history far enough, the lines begin to blur. However, by the time of the Shang dynasty, a much clearer picture begins to form. The Shang dynasty is said to have begun in 1600 BCE, and it ended around 1046 BCE. The Shang dynasty marks an important period in Chinese history, for it was at this time that the Chinese first began to think of themselves as a polity with a unique purpose.

The notion of China being the "Middle Kingdom," located at the heart of the world, began to take shape. Call it delusions of grandeur or perhaps just wishful thinking, but the idea of the Middle Kingdom states that China is at the center of it all, with the rest of the world revolving around it. The Shang dynasty might seem more than a little boastful in making these proclamations, but its rulers had a good reason to be so proud.

The Chinese under the Shang dynasty pushed the boundaries of the known world. Rulers and court astronomers tracked Mars, comets, and celestial events using inscribed oracle bones, hinting at an early scientific curiosity. Their chariots thundered across the battlefield, wielded by a class of warriors armed with gleaming bronze spears, axes, dagger-axes, and composite bows.

Bronze was the Shang's signature metal. It was used not only for warfare but also for rituals. Elaborate bronze vessels—gū goblets, jué pouring cups, and ding cauldrons—were cast with stunning precision and adorned with mythic motifs. These objects were used in ancestor worship and sacrificial rites. They were often inscribed with clan marks or short dedications. While everyday tools were still made from stone, shell, or wood, the presence of bronze objects—even if reserved for rituals or the elite—shows the Shang dynasty's ability to mobilize resources and skilled labor on an impressive scale.[i]

---

[i] Min, Anchee. *China: People, Place, Culture, History.* Pg. 83.

The Houmuwu ding, made in the 12th century during the late Shang period. This is the largest Bronze Age bronzeware that has been found anywhere in the world. It weighs almost two thousand pounds.[4]

However, perhaps the most important thing for Chinese history was the invention of writing. Archaeologists have dug up bones that contain inscriptions with Chinese characters. Referred to as "oracle bones," it is believed these artifacts were used as a form of divination.

The Shang period also crafted the first major form of religion in China by recognizing Shangdi. According to ancient Chinese tradition, Shangdi was said to have been a divine figure and the ruler of the universe. The concept of Shangdi had a monotheistic bent, even though there were lesser supernatural forces acknowledged in the Chinese pantheon. However, none could compare to Shangdi. Later Christian missionaries referred to the Christian God of the Bible as Shangdi in order to make the religion more appealing to the Chinese. Such tactics were common enough among Christians and had been carried out in other times and places.

The Chinese who revered Shangdi placed sacrifices of food, wine, and other items on altars. They did this not just out of reverence but also out of fear. They thought that if they did not constantly place sacrifices on their altars to appease Shangdi, a calamity (such as a great flood) might happen. And when things got really bad, such as in times of great crisis and upheaval, human beings were sacrificed on the altar of Shangdi in the hopes that it would stave off disaster.

The oracle bones demonstrated more than just contemplation of the heavens. The oracle bones left a clear testament to the Shang rulers' earthly power. The names of various rulers of the Shang dynasty were inscribed on these bones. When archaeologists dug up these bones, they were able to cross-check the inscribed names with later written records to verify both the authenticity of the bones and the authenticity of the preserved, written chronology of the Shang emperors.

At one point in time, the Shang dynasty had its naysayers. There were those who believed that the Shang dynasty was also, or at least partially, a product of ancient myth-making. The oracle bones prove otherwise.

The Shang dynasty was ultimately overtaken by the Zhou dynasty. The Zhou had their own complex ideas on religion and political leadership. These ideas coalesced into the concept of the Mandate of Heaven, the notion that political leaders have been given a mandate from the heavens to rule. The Zhou kickstarted a line of divine rulers who were known as the "Sons of Heaven" or "Tianzi."

During this period, the Chinese believed their own earthly ruler basically served as a bridge between the affairs of mortal humans and the heavens. The Zhou insisted that the Shang rulers had ended their reign due to their own corruption. They believed the Shang rulers had failed in what should have been their most important role—a divine intermediary.

The Zhou claimed they would be able to fulfill that role and bring peace and order to the land.

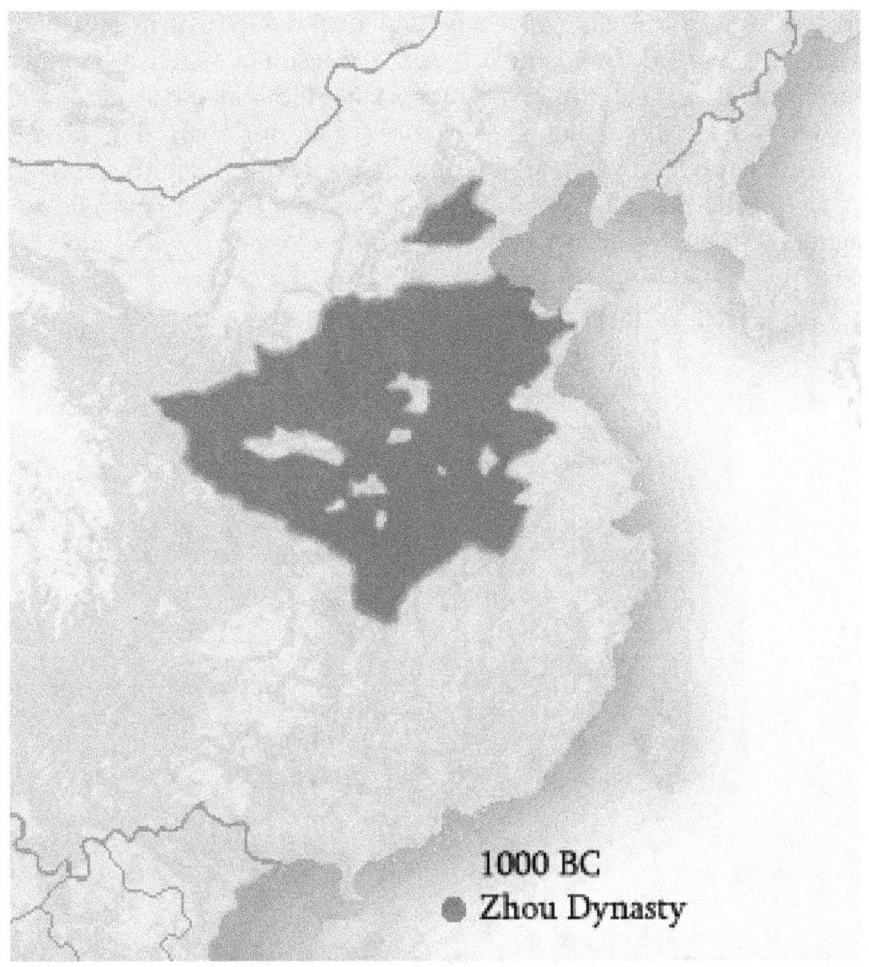

The Zhou dynasty in 1000 BCE.[5]

The aspirations of the Zhou were indeed great, as they desired to have an expansive empire with a strong centralized rule. But as much as they might have desired this kind of arrangement, the reality was far different. The Zhou dynasty was more of a confederation of feudal polities than a unified realm with a strong central government. Local leaders did see the Zhou ruler as their overlord and paid homage to him, but they otherwise lorded over their little corners of the kingdom on their own accord.

The Zhou dynasty eventually began to unravel in the 5th century BCE. Lesser lords, no longer content to pay tribute or defer to the Zhou monarch, began asserting more and more power for themselves. As these regional powers clashed for dominance, China descended into a brutal and prolonged conflict known as the Warring States period.

It was during this time of chaos and uncertainty that a man named Confucius emerged. Arguably China's greatest philosopher, Confucius started out as a keen observer of society. He looked around at the disorder and sought a solution. His answer? Restore harmony through a strict moral code and clearly defined social roles. He believed that everyone had a place, from rulers to servants, and that peace would come when people acted with virtue and fulfilled their duties.

The Warring States period.*

After centuries of warfare, one state rose above the rest. The Qin, led by a determined and ruthless ruler named Zhao Zheng, began conquering its rivals one by one. Zhao Zheng had become king of Qin at a young age following the death of his father, King Zhuangxiang, in 246 BCE. Because of his youth, power initially rested in the hands of a regent named Lu Buwei. That didn't last, though. Lu Buwei fell from grace after being caught up in a scandal; he was reportedly involved in an affair with the queen dowager.

Zhao Zheng eventually took full control and proved to be a master of statecraft and war. By 221 BCE, he had succeeded in unifying the warring states under a single ruler. He declared himself Qin Shi Huangdi—"First Emperor of Qin"—and founded a new dynasty.

Qin Shi Huangdi's regime didn't follow Confucian ideals. Instead, it embraced a strict philosophy known as Legalism. Legalist thinkers, especially Han Fei, argued that people could not be trusted to behave morally on their own. Only through harsh laws, strict punishments, and total control could order be maintained. This approach fit well with the authoritarian style of the emperor, who was not shy about using force to get his way.

Under Qin rule, sweeping reforms were introduced. There were standardized weights and measures, a unified script, a national road system, and the early construction of the Great Wall. However, the Qin dynasty's harshness also led to unrest. After Qin Shi Huangdi's death, rebellions erupted, and by 202 BCE, the dynasty was overthrown. In its place rose the Han dynasty, which would go on to rule for centuries and take a much more balanced view between Confucian morality and state power.

Chapter 3: Silk and the Sword

"Soldiers are the foundation of an army; unless they are imbued with a progressive political spirit, and unless such a spirit is fostered through progressive political work, it will be impossible to achieve genuine unity between officers and men, impossible to arouse their enthusiasm for the war of resistance to the full, and impossible to provide an excellent basis for the most effective use of all of our technical equipment and tactics."

-*Mao Zedong*[1]

Liu Bang's rise is the ultimate underdog story. Born into a peasant family in Pei County and once serving as a low-level law enforcer, few could have predicted his ascent. His leap from obscurity began when, as a Qin prison supervisor, he let prisoners escape rather than let them die under draconian laws. He fled with them, becoming an outlaw, although he eventually returned to Pei. One legend even tells how he slew a great white serpent on the road, which convinced villagers he was destined for greatness.

Fast forward a bit, and he attended the "Feast at Swan Goose Gate" in 206 BCE. This banquet was a trap set by his rival, Xiang Yu. Liu Bang slipped out alive, thanks to a mix of luck, nerves, and quick thinking.

The three-way struggle for China's future culminated in the Battle of Gaixia in 202 BCE, where Liu Bang, aided by brilliant generals like Han Xin, crushed Xiang Yu and emerged as the uncontested master of the realm. He then founded the Han dynasty.

---

[1] Zedong, Mao. *Quotations from Chairman Mao Tse-Tung (The Little Red Book)*. 1964. Pg. 80.

As emperor, Liu Bang did something unexpected. He blended strict Legalist methods with the gentler tones of Confucian thought. Though initially inclined toward realism and practicality, he was swayed by Confucian advisers like Lu Jia to soften punishments and honor ritual and moral governance. In fact, he even paid tribute to Confucius once, passing through the philosopher's hometown.

Liu Bang eventually made Chang'an, near the banks of the Wei River, his capital. This site was actually near the ruined wreckage of the previous Qin capital, Xianyang. The Han dynasty ended up being quite successful, lasting from 202 BCE to 220 CE. The Silk Road stretched all the way into the depths of the Roman Empire. Roman historian Pliny the Elder once remarked in the 1ˢᵗ century CE about how Roman citizens had become rather fond of the flow of goods from China.

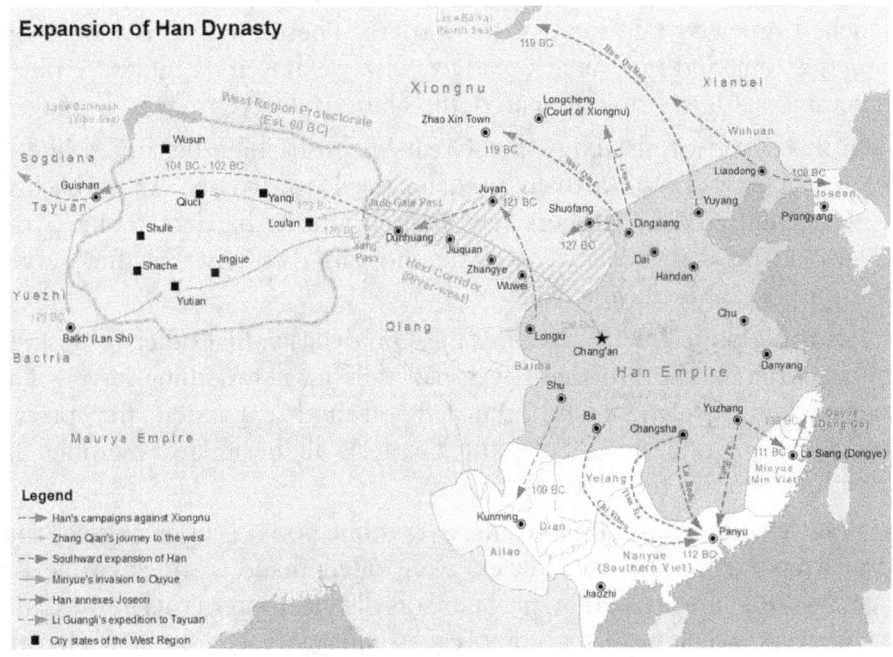

The expansion of the Han dynasty.⁷

It was not always easy going down the Silk Road, though. In 147 BCE, for example, Emperor Wudi of China decided that the merchant classes that profited from the Silk Road had gotten too rich. He decided to curtail the flow of trade down the Silk Road to stop them from gaining more influence and wealth. He also managed to capitalize on the nation's natural resources, making sure that commodities such as iron and salt were used to enrich government coffers.

During the Han dynasty, the Chinese sense of identity really began to crystallize as a distinct and separate entity, set apart from the surrounding peoples. Even today, the majority ethnic group in China is still referred to as "Han" Chinese.

After Emperor Wudi's death, the Han dynasty began its long decline. By the 2nd century CE, cracks were showing in the empire's foundations. The merchant class had grown more powerful, and with that power came greed. Speculation, especially over grain, spun out of control. Prices soared, the ordinary people suffered, and social unrest began bubbling beneath the surface.

But the problems were not just economic. While the Han were dealing with turmoil at home, the empire's northern frontier was under constant threat. Nomadic groups—first the Xiongnu, then the rising Xianbei—launched repeated raids across the borders. These incursions were more than just hit-and-run attacks; they also exposed China's growing vulnerability. Once firm and feared, the Han's military grip was slipping.

In this storm of instability, the Great Wall of China became a line of defense. The wall itself actually predates the Han dynasty. As far back as the 7th century BCE, villagers had built primitive barriers to keep out raiders. These early walls were crude and varied widely, but they served their purpose, at least for a while.

It was not until 221 BCE, under the Qin dynasty, that officials began to connect and standardize these regional walls into something larger. The Han picked up where the Qin left off and expanded the project dramatically. Under their rule, the Great Wall began to resemble the iconic structure we recognize today.

Wall sections were built using a combination of brick, stone, and compacted earth. The outer layers were often made of brick, while the core was filled with tightly packed soil. Even more crucial were the watchtowers, which were spaced at regular intervals along the wall's length. These towers allowed sentries to keep a sharp eye on the horizon. They were ready to light signal fires at the first sign of trouble.

Still, walls alone could not save an empire. However, the Han dynasty's real undoing came from within, not from outside. The economy was off-balance, the pressure on the frontier was constant, and the government was losing its grip. By the late 2nd century CE, those major cracks turned into full fractures. The Yellow Turban Rebellion broke out in 184 CE. This was a massive uprising led by desperate peasants and disillusioned commoners. Though the rebellion was crushed, it left the empire broken. In the years that followed, palace intrigues, corruption, and power struggles tore the court apart.

By 220 CE, the Han dynasty had finally fallen. The emperor was little more than a figurehead, and warlords had carved China into their own personal territories.

This is a pattern that has been repeated throughout Chinese history. Centralized power holds for a time, only to give way to regional fragmentation and civil war. From the fall of the Han to the rise of the Chinese Communist Party in the 20th century, this cycle—unity, decline, disunity, and reunification—has played out again and again.

In any case, as it pertained to the Han dynasty, centralized power broke down, and various regional powers began to duke it out. The powerbrokers of this struggle were warlords with their own regional armies, which they used to exert their will. Among them was a warlord by the name of Cao Cao. He seized control of much of northern China and laid the foundation for the Cao Wei state. He was an intriguing figure who knew as much about poetry as he did war.

Cao Cao actually began his career as a court insider of the Han dynasty. At one point, he even served as security chief under the Han, giving him great insight into the security apparatus of the Han state. He consolidated a lot of power toward the end of the Han dynasty, forging his own army of loyal troops. By the 190s, Han Emperor Xian had basically become a puppet of Cao Cao, making him a mere figurehead.

As what was left of the core of the old Han dynasty stumbled forward, Cao Cao made a name for himself. His greatest success was the unification of northern China, which he brought about in 207 CE. This unified region of northern China would become Cao Cao's personal fief, with Cao Cao essentially becoming a regional warlord, based out of this part of China, before his own passing in March of 220 CE.

His son, Cao Pi, went even further, kickstarting the short-lived Wei dynasty based in the region of northern China that his father had subdued. It was short-lived because shortly after Cao Pi was declared the supreme leader of China (forcing Emperor Xian to abdicate), two rival warlords rose up—one in the interior of China and the other in the south. These three kingdoms were Cao Wei, Shu Han, and Eastern Wu. This era came to be known as the Three Kingdoms period—one of the most legendary and turbulent times in Chinese history. It was a time of almost constant conflict, as each kingdom vied for control over a fractured China.

Each of these kingdoms had its strengths, but none could gain the upper hand for very long. War was relentless, and countless lives were lost in the pursuit of dominance. Plots, betrayals, and last-minute reversals were the norm. If this sounds like something straight out of a novel, that is because it later became one. *Romance of the Three Kingdoms* was one of China's most famous works of historical fiction, and it immortalized this era.

After decades of stalemates, one kingdom finally pulled ahead: Cao Wei. However, just when it seemed poised to reunite China, its own internal power struggles led to its undoing. A powerful general named Sima Yan eventually usurped the throne. In 266 CE, he founded a new dynasty called the Jin.

The Jin dynasty conquered Eastern Wu by 280 CE, finally reuniting the country after nearly a century of division. For a brief moment, it looked like peace had returned.

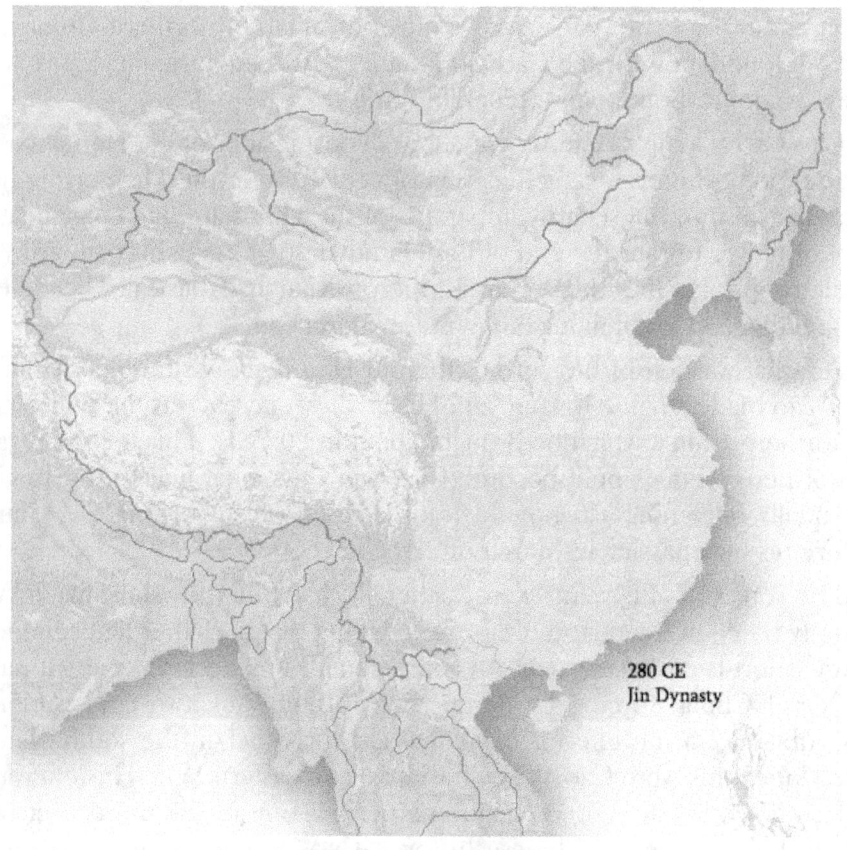

The Jin dynasty in 280 CE.'

However, we should keep in mind that one has to be careful when speaking of the Jin dynasty since there has been more than one of them during the course of China's history. About a thousand years after this first Jin dynasty, another one would rise up. This second one is often referred to as the Jurchen Jin dynasty to avoid confusion.

Just a few years after China was unified, the dynasty was dragged into a devastating internal conflict known as the War of the Eight Princes. As the dynasty tore itself apart from the inside, opportunistic groups from the north and west began pouring into China's heartland. These groups—often referred to as the Five Barbarians—included nomadic tribes like the Xiongnu, Xianbei, Di, Jie, and Qiang. They had been living along the borders for generations, sometimes under Chinese control. With the empire distracted, they seized their moment. Some rebelled, and others carved out their own small kingdoms.

In 311 CE, one of these groups stormed the Jin capital of Luoyang in what became known as the Disaster of Yongjia. The city was burned, its people were massacred, and the imperial tombs were looted. A few years later, in 316, the emperor was captured and executed. The Western Jin dynasty was over.

However, the dynasty was not quite finished. Members of the Jin royal family who survived fled south, regrouped, and set up a new capital in Jiankang—modern-day Nanjing. This was the start of the Eastern Jin dynasty. While they never recovered the northern territories, the Eastern Jin held on in the south for another century, although it was not easy. The court was riddled with intrigue. Generals and ministers constantly jockeyed for control. Still, they managed a few major victories, most notably the Battle of Fei River in 383 CE, where a much smaller Jin force defeated a powerful northern invader and saved the south from conquest.

Even the Eastern Jin could not hold on. A general named Liu Yu rose through the ranks. He outmaneuvered his rivals and took the throne in 420. He ended the Jin dynasty and started one of his own: the Liu Song dynasty. China once again slipped into a familiar pattern of rival dynasties in the north and south, each claiming legitimacy but unable to fully defeat the other.

Nearly a century later, something changed. In the south, a new emperor came to power: Emperor Wu of the Liang dynasty, who ruled from 502 to 549. He was different. Raised in the traditions of Confucianism, he later became one of China's greatest Buddhist patrons.

Known as the Bodhisattva Emperor, he poured resources into temples, encouraged the spread of Buddhist teachings, and even abolished the death penalty for a time. Under his reign, the south experienced a rare moment of peace and cultural flourishing.

It would not last forever—nothing ever does in history—but for a brief time, it looked like China might find balance again.

The fact that Buddhism took root in China is interesting. On the surface, many of the tenets of Buddhism seem incompatible with the social template provided by Confucianism. Buddhism focuses on seeking the salvation of the individual, paying no heed to social and familial ties, whereas social and family hierarchy are of great importance in Confucianism. So, how did Buddhism manage to find such fertile ground in China?

The fact that China had been politically fractured for so long likely had a lot to do with it. There was no strong Confucian-oriented polity for much of this period that could have better resisted the pull of Buddhism. Instead, in this time of chaos and upheaval, the Buddhist ideals of empowering oneself to find spiritual freedom had likely become very appealing to the people.

Another interesting aspect was that the Buddhist example of monastic life became preferable during war and violence since the monastery represented a refuge of peace and security. Religious seekers, as well as intellectuals of all kinds, found a safe and welcoming environment among the Buddhists.

Buddhist monasteries eventually became more than just religious centers. They were also educational centers, safeguarding Chinese intellectual thought and culture. The manner in which Buddhist monasteries became centers of education during these troubling times in China's history has some historical parallels. The safeguarding of knowledge in Buddhist monasteries is very similar to the way in which Christian monasteries served as beacons of spiritual and intellectual light during the European Dark Ages. As the warlords duked it out during this troubling period in China, the safest place to deposit books, manuscripts, inventions, or any other notable ideas was likely in a Buddhist monastery.

The Hanging Monastery in Shanxi Province.[9]

Out of this tumult came the Sui dynasty, which was briefly prominent, lasting from 581 to 618. The Sui dynasty was a mere speedbump in the long history of China, but it was important all the same. Under the Sui, the rulers again unified China. Although the dynasty lasted fewer than forty years, it laid out the framework for a much more successful dynasty: the Tang.

Chapter 4: From the Tang to the Song

"Life is really simple, but men insist on making it complicated."
-Confucius[i]

The great Emperor Gaozu founded the Tang dynasty around 618. He was initially struggling for dominance in a competitive field of candidates who were seeking to lead the flailing Sui dynasty. He ultimately put down his rivals, but instead of continuing the Sui dynasty, he forged the Tang dynasty instead. The Tang built upon the Sui and managed to create lasting legal codes and government infrastructure.

Emperor Gaozu's government was not a one-man show. It operated through a clever structure known as the Three Departments and Six Ministries. Think of it as a high-functioning administration: one department drafted policy, another reviewed it, and a third carried it out. Meanwhile, the six ministries—personnel (handling appointments), revenue (managing taxes and finance), rites (dealing with ceremonies and protocols), war (military affairs), justice (law and order), and works (infrastructure)—handled the day-to-day running of the empire.

Now, about the royal drama. Gaozu's two most formidable sons were Li Jiancheng, the crown prince, and Li Shimin, the warrior prince. Unlike Li Jiancheng, who spent much of his time stationed on the frontier,

---

[i] Brewer, D. *Quotes of Confucius and Their Interpretations: A Words of Wisdom Collection Book.* Pg. 39.

Li Shimin was the empire's hero, defeating key rivals and commanding respect from the army. The competition between them was fierce, and it eventually boiled over into open violence.

In 626, that tension came to a head in what's now known as the Xuanwu Gate Incident. Li Shimin set an ambush at the palace's northern gate and assassinated Li Jiancheng and their brother, Li Yuanji. It was quick, brutal, and effective. Within days, Emperor Gaozu had no choice but to make Li Shimin the crown prince, and soon after, he abdicated in his favor.

Li Shimin became Emperor Taizong, and he went on to become one of China's greatest rulers. Taizong was known to have greatly projected Chinese power. He managed to expand his territory and create satellite vassals out of neighboring countries. He even made inroads in the Tarim Basin, reaching into central Asia. Here, the Tang managed to bring the Uyghurs and Turkish nomads to heel, thereby securing the Silk Road.

Interestingly, Emperor Taizong's sister, Princess Pingyang, is said to have played a big role in all of this. She was apparently skilled in the art of war. In what was most certainly an unusual development back in those days, Princess Pingyang actually led her own battalion of troops, which was known as the Army of the Lady. This army was able to conquer a few territories of strategic importance. Princess Pingyang was then able to unite her forces with those of Emperor Taizong.

It is not entirely clear what happened to Princess Pingyang, but it is said that she perished while in her twenties in 623. Demonstrating how important she was to the Chinese war effort (not to mention how important she was to her brother), the princess was given a military burial similar to what would have been given to an accomplished male general.

This security brought more trade, and with it came a whole lot more traffic. Soon, many outsiders were flocking to China, creating a cosmopolitan feel in many Chinese cities. The influence of the Tang even managed to reach Japan, which began to actively emulate China.

China and Tibet also began to develop a close relationship around this time. Their relationship revolved around the trade of tea and horses. It sounds rather simple, and from a commerce perspective, it is. After all, China wanted horses and Tibet wanted tea. The trade route that carved its way through China into the highlands of Tibet was known as the Tea Horse Road. Of course, tea and horses were not the only things that traveled along this road. As Chinese culture mingled with Tibetan life, Buddhism took root and began to reshape Tibetan spiritual practices.

Emperor Taizong died in 649 CE, leaving the throne to his son, Gaozong. On paper, the new ruler had all the makings of a worthy successor—he had years as crown prince and a fine education, plus the Tang dynasty was at its height. Yet in the eyes of later chroniclers, Gaozong was a shadow of his father. They painted him as hesitant, pliable, and all too easily swayed by his brilliant and ambitious consort, Wu Zetian, a woman who had once served as Taizong's concubine. That single fact was enough for later storytellers to cast his reign as ineffective, turning a court romance into a political cautionary tale.

However, this was not just mere slander because his taking up with Wu Zetian did have a big impact on his reign. Even though Gaozong was already married, this concubine managed to become Gaozong's favorite. Demonstrating a more powerful sense of willpower than Gaozong could muster, she managed to convince him to recognize her as more or less an equal.

As such, this former concubine became the infamous Empress Wu, and soon she—not Gaozong—was the true power behind the throne. Gaozong eventually became incapacitated by a stroke, and Empress Wu served as his "interpreter." No one could understand the stricken Gaozong but the empress. This was very convenient for her, although it was inconvenient for everyone else. She basically made Gaozong her own feeble puppet. Empress Wu could propose any policy she wanted. During these dark days, she made sure that her and Gaozong's son were established as the heirs to the throne, thereby ensuring her own hold on the Tang dynasty.

Although Gaozong's reign was troubled, the empire was still strong thanks to his predecessor. The Tang Empire had expanded geographically, absorbing plenty of additional resources. The army had also expanded and was a formidable fighting force, no matter who was on the throne.

In fact, the military might of China beckoned a horde of refugees from Persia (modern-day Iran) who were fleeing from the Islamic conquest. The Persians had an ancient empire; by the 7th century, the empire already stretched back thousands of years. However, at the start of Gaozong's reign, Persia was overwhelmed by the determined and ideologically empowered Arab army. Persian defenses were ultimately overrun.

After the fall of the Sasanian Empire in 651, members of the royal Persian family fled east, seeking refuge from the Arab conquest. Among them was Peroz, a son of the last Sasanian king, Yazdegerd III. He made his way to Tang China, where he and other Persian nobles were welcomed by the emperor and granted titles and protection.

Some later stories even claim that one of Yazdegerd's daughters entered the Tang imperial court, possibly as a concubine to Emperor Taizong, though this part of the tale is steeped more in legend than documented fact.

Under Tang protection, Peroz lived out his days in the Chinese borderlands. Though he likely harbored dreams of one day returning to reclaim his homeland, that dream never materialized. Over time, the Persian refugees chose to settle, raise families, and gradually integrate into Chinese society. It is said that near the end of his life, Peroz advised his people to honor their Persian roots while embracing the land that had sheltered them.

And so they did. Over generations, through intermarriage and cultural exchange, this Persian community became woven into the broader fabric of Chinese civilization. Today, only subtle traces remain.

Emperor Gaozong died in 683, and just as Empress Wu had arranged, the heir was her son with Gaozong, Zhongzong. If she expected a pliable figurehead, she was soon disappointed. When Zhongzong began to assert himself, favoring his wife's family over Empress Wu's influence, she moved swiftly. She deposed him after barely six weeks and installed her younger son, Ruizong, on the throne. Empress Wu ruled in all but name.

For years, she kept up the appearance of Tang rule, but in 690, she cast aside the pretense. She declared herself emperor and made the empire her own. She served as the sole authority of China over the next fifteen years. Even though Empress Wu is widely reviled in traditional Chinese history, one could argue that she was, in fact, a fairly decent ruler. Yes, her climb to power was ruthless, but she played the game of politics remarkably well. Rising from concubine to emperor, she inherited a shaky dynasty and turned it into a flourishing one. She got rid of corruption, expanded the empire, rejuvenated the economy, and transformed the civil service so that ability, not birth, became the measure of a man.

Just before her death in 705, Wu Zetian was forced by illness and palace intrigue to reinstate her son Zhongzong. However, Zhongzong's second go at ruling would not work out very well at all. Zhongzong's death in 710 CE was sudden and widely believed to be no accident. Traditional historians say Empress Wei, backed by her daughter Princess Anle, poisoned him with a cake. She wanted to follow the path of previous empresses and seize true power herself. With the emperor gone, Wei enthroned his young son, Li Chongmao, hoping he would be a puppet under her thumb.

However, this was not how things played out. Within two weeks, a coup led by Zhongzong's sister, Princess Taiping, and Li Dan's son, the future Xuanzong, overthrew Empress Wei. Ruizong, Zhongzong's brother, was put on the throne, and the coup plotters were executed.

Emperor Xuanzong would have a much more stable rule than his immediate predecessors. He led the dynasty from 712 to 756; his reign was the longest among the Tang emperors. However, his reign was not without its problems. Middle Eastern armies, fueled by the fervor of Islam, were on the march. Persia had already been knocked out, and now Islamic ideologues were hammering at China's own western borderlands.

Emperor Xuanzong's later years took an unexpected turn. His most cherished companion was Consort Wu, a great-niece of the formidable Empress Wu Zetian. When she died suddenly in 737, Xuanzong was inconsolable. In his grief, his affections turned to an unlikely figure: the young wife of his own son, Prince Shou. To make the match possible, she briefly donned Taoist robes to dissolve her marriage. Then, she returned to the palace as Yang Guifei.

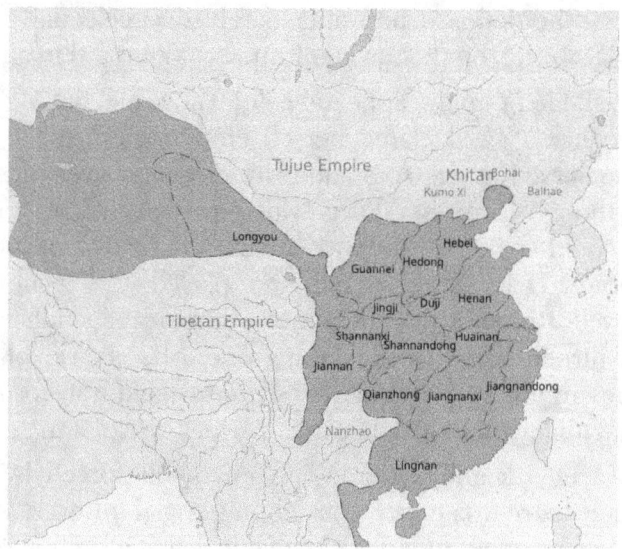

The Tang dynasty in the early 740s.[10]

The Tang army was in for a stunning defeat. In 751, an Arab army from the Abbasid Caliphate confronted Tang forces near the banks of the Talas River, which flows through Kyrgyzstan and Kazakhstan. For the Tang, the battle would mark the end of their western ambitions. Midway through the fight, their Turkic Karluk allies—said to number some twenty thousand—suddenly turned their lances against the Chinese, joining their Muslim brethren in crushing the Tang. When the dust settled, the Abbasids held the field, and Tang influence beyond the Tian Shan, a mountain range in central Asia, was gone for good.

This was a stunning blow to China. The real shock came in 755 when General An Lushan rose up in rebellion and seized both of the Tang capitals. Xuanzong fled for his life. In the chaos, his son, Li Heng, was proclaimed Emperor Suzong in the north. Xuanzong formally abdicated, though he still issued decrees for a short while.

With the empire on the brink of collapse, Suzong made a desperate but effective move. He called in the Uyghur Khaganate. These mounted warriors answered the call and helped the Tang army reclaim Chang'an and Luoyang in late 757. This alliance saved the dynasty, but it came at a cost. Suzong's reliance on foreign troops revealed just how fragile imperial power had become.

The Uyghurs had recently accepted Islam and were among the many warring tribes on the steppes at that time. The Uyghurs were skilled warriors, even on horseback, making them a highly mobile and valuable strike force to the Chinese. The Uyghurs helped the Chinese retake some lost territories, but in exchange for their efforts, thousands of Uyghurs were allowed to settle in the far reaches of northwestern China in what today is referred to as Xiangjiang province. Both the region and the Uyghurs themselves have been in the news headlines of more recent times due to accusations that the Chinese are attempting a cultural (if not a literal) genocide against the Uyghurs. They have forbidden the practice of Islam and forced the Uyghurs to adopt Chinese customs and ideological beliefs. There is still much debate on what may or may not be taking place in Xiangjiang.

China might have managed to secure its borders during this period, but more internal problems were to come. China entered into what is historically known as the Late Tang Weak Monsoon Period. This was a roughly one-hundred-year-long cycle of extreme drought, which led to crop failures. As is often the case, during this time of crisis, the social order broke down, and rebellions and insurrections became frequent.

In 878, the Chinese rebel leader Huang Chao launched a devastating uprising against the Tang dynasty. Part of his anger was channeled toward foreign communities—Muslims, Jews, Christians, and Zoroastrians—who became scapegoats for China's troubles. Huang's forces stormed Guangzhou. Historians from the Persian Gulf estimated that tens of thousands of foreigners were slaughtered, though Chinese records are quieter about the numbers.

Huang's rebellion shook the empire to its core. Eventually, the Tang court enlisted new military talent, most notably the Shatuo leader Li Keyong, to crush the rebellion. By 884, Huang had been defeated, but the dynasty was a shadow of its former self. Over the following decades, regional military governors gained influence, and the central authority continued to weaken until the Tang dynasty finally ended in 907.

Out of that chaos, the Five Dynasties and Ten Kingdoms period began. It was not until 960 that peace—and a new dynasty—returned. Zhao Kuangyin, later Emperor Taizu of the Song, rose to unify the realm and establish the Song dynasty, which would endure until 1279.

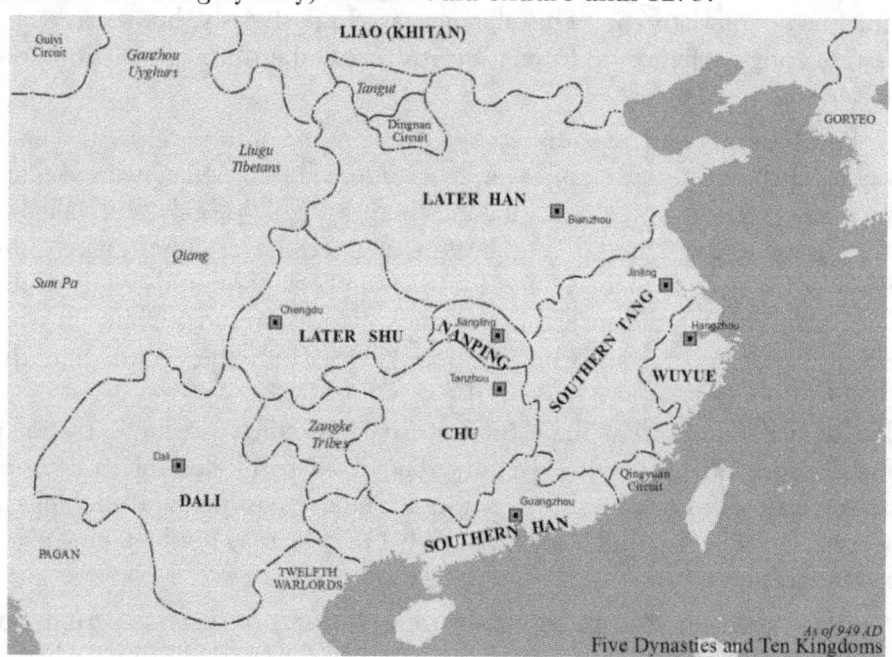

A map of China during the Five Dynasties and Ten Kingdoms period.[11]

The Song dynasty was shaped in no small part by the nomadic warriors of the northern steppes. Their influence was both direct and indirect. Once the empire was unified under Zhao Kuangyin, its rulers looked to the north, determined to secure the frontier against Khitan and Tangut raids. Garrisons were strengthened, and troops were stationed in force along the borders. However, this was a costly and unsustainable policy. Before long, the Song abandoned the idea of holding the line through sheer force of arms, choosing instead to buy peace with silk, silver, and gold.

This practice is also not sustainable. The more you pay someone not to attack you, the more threats and attacks there are so that the aggressor can get an even bigger payout from you.

After decades of skirmishes along their shaky northern border, the Song dynasty finally agreed to peace in 1005 by signing the Chanyuan Treaty with the Khitan-led Liao dynasty. The Song agreed to pay an annual tribute of silk and silver and formally recognize the Liao as equals. In return, there would be decades of peace, which allowed the Song to focus on culture, education, and the economy.

The Leifeng Pagoda by Li Song.[13]

Within the borders of the Song dynasty, a kind of renaissance was taking place. Despite the turbulence outside, the arts flourished, and there were innovative inventions of all kinds. The Song Empire developed a practical military use of gunpowder, refined the compass, and issued true paper money (a first in world history). The Song also greatly expanded the civil service, creating a complex bureaucracy. Those interested in civil service positions had to take exams. They had to demonstrate their ability to write essays, their knowledge of Confucian principles, and even write their own poetry. This introduced the idea that one could rise through the ranks by way of merit. One's background was important, but if one could not apply practical knowledge to their position, then they were not the right candidate.

It was a nice idea, but much of the time, it did not actually work in practice. There was still an awful lot of corruption, which served to aid some over others. There were also segments of the Chinese population who were illiterate, such as laborers or farmers, who simply did not have the education necessary to take a civil examination in the first place. Nevertheless, the Chinese civil service and its exams were a unique and forward-thinking innovation at the time.

During the Song dynasty, China developed a great passion for theater. Playhouses popped up in just about every city, and actors portrayed dramas of all kinds.

None of these dramas could compete with the very real drama taking shape in China's northern frontier. As northern China became less prosperous and more unpredictable, southern China (later known as the Southern Song dynasty) rose to prominence. In the south, rice and tea were produced in large quantities. This led to a shift away from the previous diet of mostly grains to one centered around the foodstuffs of southern China. Rice could be grown in the warm climate of southern China and then shipped via waterways to the major cities farther north, keeping everyone well fed.

In the early 1100s, the Song struck a risky bargain with the rising Jurchens. Together, they would crush the Khitan Liao dynasty. The Jin dynasty, as the Jurchens styled themselves, swept the Khitans from the map by 1125 and then turned their armies south. In 1127, they stormed the Song capital at Kaifeng, carrying off the emperor and his court in what became known as the Jingkang Incident. The Northern Song was gone. The remnants of the dynasty fled south, eventually establishing a new capital at Hangzhou. From there, the Southern Song would endure for another century and a half until the Mongols came to finish its story in 1279.

Ever since their great progenitor Genghis Khan rose to prominence in Mongolia in 1206, the Mongols had been on the march. His grandson, Kublai Khan, would defeat Song China and establish a unified China under his own rule, which would become known as the Yuan dynasty.

Although the Yuan dynasty was a Mongol creation, it did what it could to replicate the achievements of the Song.

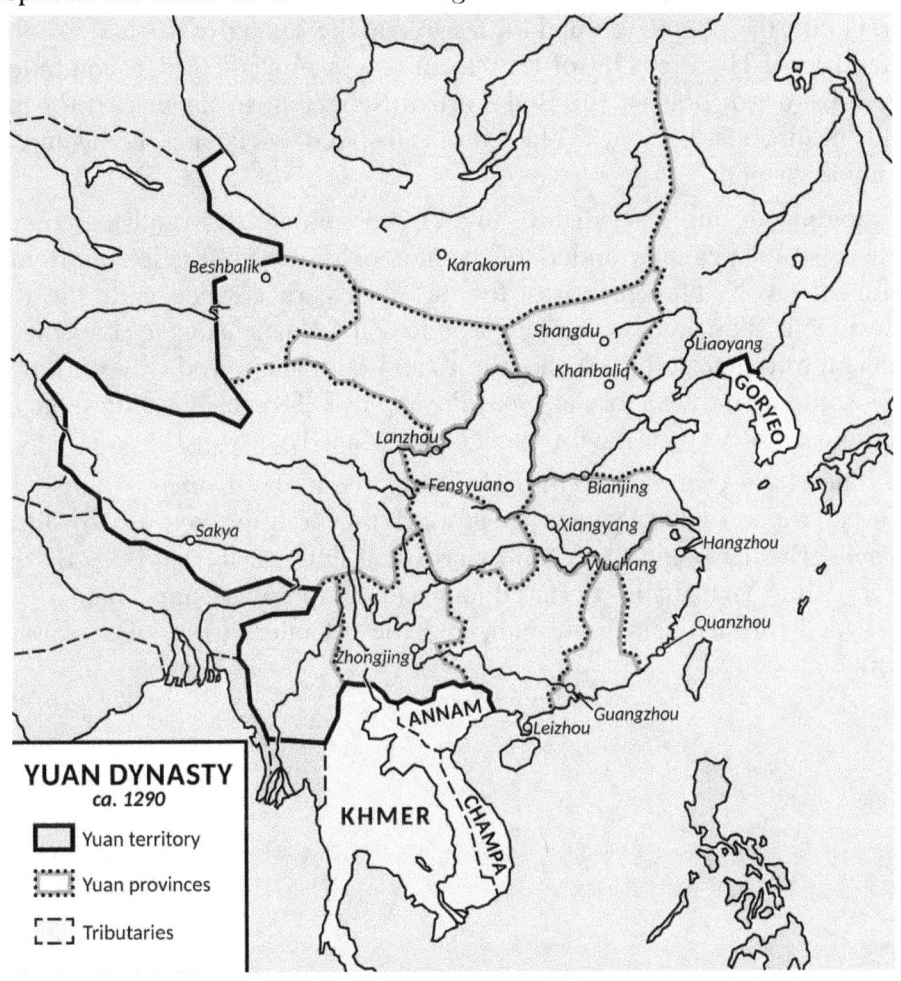

The Yuan dynasty.[18]

The Mongols took advantage of Song achievements, such as paper money and gunpowder. Despite their fearsome reputation, the Mongols were not necessarily malevolent overlords. Life for most Chinese went on as usual. Even so, there was growing resentment over the fact that China was being run by outsiders.

The Chinese soon began moving toward open revolt against their Mongol rulers. During this time of duress, many delved into mysticism and prophecy, seeking a sign that an intervention against the Mongols might be at hand. Although it is debatable what this "sign" could be, there was one incident in particular that stood out.

In the 1350s, China was battered by harsh climates, crop failures, floods, cyclones, famine, and possibly even plague. Disillusioned and desperate, the people yearned for a sign that the Yuan dynasty had lost the Mandate of Heaven. Out of this storm rose a movement that combined spirituality with politics: the Red Turban Rebellion. It was named for the red headbands tied by White Lotus-inspired sectarians preaching a coming savior.

Starting around 1351, figures like Han Shantong began rallying corvée laborers and peasants under the banner of divine restoration and anti-Mongol revolt. Though it was, for the most part, crushed early on, the movement ultimately coalesced around Zhu Yuanzhang, a charismatic general who defeated the Yuan armies and outmaneuvered rival warlords. His stunning naval victory at Lake Poyang in 1363 sealed his dominance and paved the way for the founding of the Ming dynasty in 1368.

The chaos even spilled into Goryeo (present-day Korea), where Red Turban forces raided Pyongyang, although they were pushed back by local armies. By that point, the Yuan dynasty had little left to stand on. By the time Zhu Yuanzhang declared himself emperor, China had been reshaped through rebellion, faith, and the relentless force of a peasant army.

Chapter 5: The Majesty of the Ming Dynasty

"In seeking victory, those who direct a war cannot overstep the limitations imposed by the objective conditions. Within these limitations, however, they can and must play a dynamic role in striving for victory. The stage of action for commanders in a war must be built upon objective possibilities, but on that stage they can direct the performance of many a drama, full of sound and color, power and grandeur."

-Mao Zedong[i]

The revolt that pushed the Mongols out of China was led by Zhu Yuanzhang. Zhu was an unlikely hero in many respects, and he was most certainly an unlikely leader. He was an orphan and had lived most of his life as a homeless vagabond. He eventually adopted Buddhism and depended upon the kindness of strangers for sustenance.

During his days as a wandering Buddhist monk, he happened upon a religious and political revival of sorts. This popular revival ultimately morphed into the Red Turban Rebellion. After driving the Mongols from China, Zhu formed the Ming dynasty, which roughly translates as "bringer of light." Yes, Zhu and his followers saw themselves as bringing light back to China. They restored order, virtue, and Chinese traditions after what they viewed as years of Mongol misrule.

---

[i] Zedong, Mao. *Quotations from Chairman Mao Tse-Tung (The Little Red Book)*. Pg. 124.

To many in China, especially the Confucian elite, the Yuan dynasty had been a dark chapter. China had to deal with foreign overlords, harsh taxes, and a loss of cultural identity. But in truth, the picture was more complicated. The Mongols maintained trade routes, tolerated diverse religions, and brought China into closer contact with the wider world. Even so, for many Chinese at the time, the end of the Yuan dynasty felt like the lifting of a long shadow.

Zhu Yuanzhang became the Hongwu Emperor. He was determined to bring back a renaissance of Chinese culture and innovation, which had been subsumed for so long by the Mongolian occupiers. The Hongwu Emperor also made sure to reestablish protocols with all of China's former tribute nations. He let it be known that he fully expected the leaders of China's traditional satellites to pay their respects to him personally. And they did. The first to arrive was Tran Du Tong, the emperor of Vietnam. Several other leaders from other Southeast Asian nations, such as Cambodia, Majapahit, Borneo, and Sumatra, also sent representatives.

The Hongwu Emperor orchestrated elaborate ceremonies where foreign dignitaries were received with fanfare, hospitality, and no small amount of symbolic power play. These rituals were meant to underscore China's superiority and the emperor's dominance. Visiting rulers were treated with generosity, but it was always clear that any show of disobedience would bring swift consequences.

That message applied not just to foreign emissaries but to internal threats as well. In 1380, the emperor's growing paranoia came to a head when he suspected his own chancellor, Hu Weiyong, of plotting treason. Whether the plot was real or imagined is still debated, but

Portrait of the Hongwu Emperor.[14]

what followed was a purge. Hu Weiyong was executed, and tens of thousands of officials, associates, and even distant contacts were swept up in the fallout. The office of chancellor was abolished, and from that point on, the six ministries reported directly to the emperor. The Hongwu Emperor had consolidated control in a way no Chinese emperor had before.

The emperor's paranoia extended to other parts of court life, especially the palace eunuchs. These castrated men were tasked with guarding the imperial harem since their condition eliminated any risk of scandal with the emperor's concubines. However, the Hongwu Emperor believed that physical barriers were not enough to prevent intrigue. He thought eunuchs could still conspire, especially with concubines who might use their influence for personal or political gain. There were whispers of plots, embezzlement schemes, and interference in state affairs. Whether those rumors were founded or not, Hongwu treated them seriously. In 1385, he issued a sweeping decree. Any eunuch found involved in political plotting would face immediate execution.[i]

As the end of his reign approached, the Hongwu Emperor made a bold dynastic decision. Instead of passing the throne to one of his many surviving sons, he named his young grandson, Zhu Yunwen, as his successor. He would become the Jianwen Emperor, and he came to power in 1398. Still in his teens, the Jianwen Emperor faced a fractured court and a country weary of purges and authoritarian rule. Recognizing this, his first major act as emperor was to issue a general pardon. He released many who had been imprisoned or sidelined under his grandfather's regime, offering clemency to those who had fallen out of favor. This was not just a gesture of goodwill. The Jianwen Emperor needed to stabilize the empire and win loyalty from factions still smarting from the Hongwu Emperor's reign.

But as promising as the Jianwen Emperor's reign had begun, it would end rather abruptly in 1402. The exact way in which the Jianwen Emperor was toppled remains unknown, but we have a general idea. His demise was born out of the animosity of his uncles, who were upset that they had been passed over in the line of succession. They felt that the Hongwu Emperor should never have considered his grandson; they felt that the crown should have first gone to one of the Hongwu Emperor's brothers.

---

[i] Min, Anchee. *China: People, Place, Culture, History.* Pg. 108.

One of these uncles cobbled together a large army and marched on the capital of China, Nanjing. The next thing anyone knew, Jianwen was nowhere to be seen. The uncle who had stormed into Nanjing claimed that he was on a rescue mission to save his nephew from an attempted coup. However, he then claimed that he had failed in his mission and that the young man had been killed; he was apparently burned alive in his own palace. Most could read between the lines of all this and realized that his uncle had killed him. At any rate, this uncle went on to become the Yongle Emperor. He would rule from 1402 to 1424.

The Yongle Emperor was an expansionist and built up the army so that he could fulfill his expansionist ambitions. In 1403, he moved the capital of China to Beijing. Prior to this, Nanjing was considered the capital, but shortly after coming to power, the Yongle Emperor decided that Beijing was of greater strategic importance and would be the better choice for China's capital city. If anything else, he could keep a better watch on the continued threat of Mongol invasion from Beijing.

Shortly after Beijing was designated the capital, construction began on one of China's most noteworthy sites, the Forbidden City. This inner sanctum of Beijing, said to be forbidden because it was the official stomping grounds of the emperor, would not be finalized until the year 1420.

The Yongle Emperor also did everything he could to strengthen the ancient Great Wall of China. The Great Wall had long stood as a barrier between China and invaders. The Yongle Emperor sought to bolster its potential for deterrence and defense as much as possible. In fact, the Great Wall reached its maximum length and came to take on the general design and appearance that the structure is known for today under the Ming.

One of the most endearing legacies of the wall's refurbishment during the Ming era was that towns popped up along the wall due to the tremendous manpower needed to work on the sections. These towns became lasting settlements.

The Yongle Emperor was quite enthusiastic about using the resources and manpower that China already had at its disposal, and this also extended to the Chinese army. In the past, the Chinese had relied heavily on mercenaries. The Yongle Emperor made sure that China had its own homegrown army on which it could depend.

As much as China was seeking to defend its people during this period, it was also embarking on previously unheard-of explorations. During the Ming era, the famed Admiral Zheng He led a fleet of Chinese galleons over the Indian Ocean to tour India, Africa, and everything in between.

Zheng He's first exploratory mission took place from 1405 to 1407. He and his crew traveled past Indochina and down to Java before entering the Indian Ocean. Several more voyages ensued to parts far and wide, which would be remembered by the locals for several decades.

Zheng He's ships are referred to as the "Treasure Fleets," and for good reason. These ships were loaded to the brim with all manner of goods. The Chinese wanted to make sure that they were beholden to no one during these trips, so they supplied these ships with more than just provisions. This put them in a strong position as diplomats since they could arrive at a foreign port bearing gifts and seeking nothing in return. Well, nothing, perhaps, except for a pledge of future diplomatic relations with China from their hosts.

As awed as these local leaders were by the spectacle, they could hardly say that the Chinese were threatening them or stealing their resources. So, what was it that they wanted? It seems that they wanted to spread Chinese worldviews and philosophy, not so much through force but by a gentle diplomatic push.

If this was indeed the goal, one could say that Zheng He's efforts were a stunning success. The few exotic items he returned with were a source of endless amusement and wonder in the Chinese court. For example, Zheng He's ships returned with a rather remarkable animal that most Chinese knew nothing about. They were stunned to see a beast with a tremendously long neck being led out of a ship and out onto the dock. This animal was a giraffe. This particular giraffe originally hailed from Africa but had been picked up in Bengal. The giraffe's arrival in China was well documented by paintings, poems, and chronicles.

Interestingly enough, some Chinese spoke of the animal as somehow being prophetic. This was due to the fact that Chinese myth spoke of a unicorn-like creature that was last seen during the time of Confucius. The giraffe does not really look like a unicorn, but it is possible that some Chinese thought it was weird enough to classify it as one. They insisted that its arrival in China meant that the Chinese had entered into a new and wondrous golden age. There was certainly an optimistic mood in China during the early days of the Ming dynasty.

Zheng He's last voyage ended up on the eastern coast of Africa in an apparent search for the native habitat of exotic animals like the giraffe. Diplomacy was also a part of his agenda, with Zheng He establishing diplomatic relations with regions in Southeast Asia and East Africa. But as interesting and ground-breaking as these trips were, they were determined to be a waste of money since more resources were needed to maintain northern defenses and undertake punitive expeditions against the constant threat of the Mongols.

Emperor Yongle passed away in 1424. His successor allowed one more voyage in 1431 before shutting down the Treasure Fleets for good. European explorers, in the meantime, were ramping up their own efforts at exploration, with the Portuguese leading the charge. The Portuguese would reach India in 1498, and they would reach China itself in 1514.

Just prior to this feat, the Portuguese had forcefully seized the nearby Southeast Asian island of Malacca. Malacca served as a stepping stone to reach China. As daring as the Portuguese were, they were not about to strong-arm China into submission. However, they did engage in a rather aggressive form of diplomacy. After several entreaties by the eager Portuguese, the Chinese finally allowed a Portuguese mission to be established in China's southern port city of Canton.

The Chinese had been using Canton for some time as an official weigh station and to deal with foreign delegations. The Portuguese were viewed as just the latest of these pests, but little did the Chinese know that the Portuguese were playing for keeps. Relations eventually broke down once China discovered rogue Portuguese sailors were basically resorting to piracy in Chinese waters.

These trespasses led to a confrontation between a Ming fleet and a Portuguese fleet in the vicinity of Guangzhou. The Portuguese were thrashed by the Chinese, and in the aftermath, Chinese officials sought to end all relations with them. The persistent Portuguese eventually wormed their way back. In 1554, they managed to gain permission to establish another mission, this time in the Chinese port of Macau. Macau became an official trading post in 1557. The Portuguese were thinking more about the long term than the Chinese would have guessed at the time. Macau would ultimately become a Portuguese colony; it remained a Portuguese possession until 1999.

The Portuguese were not the only Europeans who made inroads in Asia. Their Iberian cousins, the Spaniards, were not far behind. By the late 1500s, the Spaniards had conquered their way across the Americas.

After disembarking from the Pacific coast, they pushed farther west—so far west, in fact, that one could say it became east! They ultimately sailed all the way to the Philippines, which fell under their control as well.

From their base in the Philippines, the Spaniards sailed to China with galleons full of gold and silver freshly purloined from their American conquests. Chinese coffers would become filled with Spanish silver, while Spanish ships were filled with silk and other precious commodities.

As much as European depredations played a role in China's later decline, during this period, China actually had more to fear from Japan. The Japanese certainly could not stand up to Ming China on a one-to-one basis militarily, but for several decades, rogue pirate bands had been plaguing the Chinese coasts. These pirates posed a significant threat to China's resources.

Matters came to a head in 1592 when Japan officially invaded Korea. At the time, Korea was a tributary vassal of China. If China could not protect its own vassal states, no one would look at China as a strong and effective power. If Korea could not count on China's protection, who could?

By the late Ming period, the cracks in the dynasty had begun to show. Years of financial strain, political corruption, and environmental disasters like floods and famines had battered the empire. Though still impressive in size and influence, the Ming government was growing weaker by the decade. The war with Japan in Korea had been a major blow. While China successfully repelled the invaders and preserved its status as protector of the Korean court, the effort drained the treasury and exposed just how fragile the Ming military machine had become.

As Ming control over its vast territories began to slip, the northeastern region of Manchuria grew increasingly independent. The Jurchen tribes of this region—later known as the Manchus—had long existed at the empire's edge. They were sometimes trading partners, but at other times, they were foes. Though they had pledged allegiance to the Ming court in earlier decades, that relationship had grown hollow. By the early 1600s, the Manchus had organized under a charismatic leader named Nurhaci, who united the Jurchen clans and declared the founding of a new state. He soon issued a manifesto—known as the Seven Grievances—which formally accused the Ming of betrayal and declared open war.

Even as the Ming grappled with this threat from the north, its internal foundations were crumbling. Court officials were locked in endless power struggles. The emperor's ear was often captured by eunuchs or self-serving ministers. Rebellions broke out across the countryside as peasants grew desperate and local governors lost control.

And yet, even in this climate of political decay, the cultural life of China remained vibrant. The late Ming period saw a flourishing of art, literature, and philosophy. Painters experimented with bold new styles, and novelists penned some of China's most enduring works. Intellectuals like Wang Yangming challenged rigid orthodoxy with calls for moral self-cultivation and inner clarity.

Eventually, the final blow came not from the Manchus directly but from within. In 1644, the rebel leader Li Zicheng stormed Beijing, and the last Ming emperor took his own life. A desperate Ming general, Wu Sangui, opened the gates of the Great Wall to the Manchus, hoping they could defeat the rebels. They did, but once the Manchus were inside, they never left. They swept through the capital and established a new dynasty, the Qing, which would rule China until the dawn of the 20th century.

Chapter 6: The Qing— China's Last Dynasty

"Your foreign ships come hither, striving the one with the other for our trade, and for the simple reason of their strong desire to reap profit. By what principle of reason, then, should these foreigners send in return a poisonous drug, which involves in destruction those very natives of China?"

-Commissioner Lin Zexu[i]

The ruling line of the Qing dynasty was rooted in the Jurchen people, who were originally semi-nomadic tribes in northeastern China and the founders of the Jin dynasty. By the 15th century, the Jurchens had become Ming tributaries. They regularly sent tribute and received titles and trade privileges. Though still officially vassals to the Ming court, their repeated interactions familiarized them with Chinese bureaucratic and military structures.

When Nurhaci rose to unify the Jianzhou Jurchen tribes, he borrowed strategically from both Ming governance and Mongol organizational methods. He formalized the Eight Banners system, creating a military and administrative framework that became the bedrock of Manchu identity and later Qing rule.

---

[i] Clements, Jonathan. *A Brief History of China.* 2019. Pg. 320.

As their ambitions grew, the Manchus expanded their army, and they relied not only on Jurchen warriors but also on defecting Han Chinese soldiers. Marriages were brokered between prominent Han officers and Manchu nobility to lock in loyalty. These alliances made it increasingly difficult for the Ming to retain loyalty among their former subjects, even though Ming leaders were slow to fully grasp the emerging threat.

The Manchu rulers treated the Chinese defectors well, valuing the military expertise they brought with them and rewarding them heartily for their contributions. Along with troops, the Manchu also recruited artisans and technicians of all sorts from China and Korea. Due to Manchu largesse, working for the Manchu soon became more appealing than working for the Ming.

In 1625, Nurhaci designated Mukden (now Shenyang) as his capital. He claimed legitimacy that was reminiscent of Chinese emperors by embracing the concept of the Mandate of Heaven. In 1616, he formally established the Later Jin state. By 1636, Nurhaci's successor, Hong Taiji, renamed the people, switching from Jurchen to Manchu, and the realm as Great Qing, cementing his broader ambitions.

Meanwhile, the Ming dynasty, though increasingly pushed southward, still ruled parts of China. While all of these maneuvers by the Manchu were being made, China was facing an economic downturn. The flow of silver from the Americas had dropped off, and market prices in China were affected. Making matters worse was a series of poor harvests due to droughts and other climatic disturbances. Revolts were common in China, and even the military could not be counted on to mount a proper defense of the realm. The Manchu knew as much. In 1644, a Manchu army poured into Beijing and took the Chinese capital without any resistance.

The Chinese emperor, whose army and advisers had abandoned him, took his own life. Even so, the Qing had trouble consolidating their power since various warlords had risen up in pockets that remained out of their reach, such as in deep southwestern China and even on the island of Taiwan.

The Qing invaded Taiwan in 1683 to stamp out the last vestige of Ming power and officially annexed the island. After the annexation of Taiwan, Qing China began to consider expanding its frontiers even further. Expansions were made into Tibet and the southwestern region of what is now called Xinjiang province.

The most effective ruler of the Qing dynasty was the Kangxi Emperor (also referred to as Emperor Shengzu of Qing). He ruled from 1661 to 1722. After China's borders were consolidated under the Kangxi Emperor, he began to reach out to the Chinese diaspora, encouraging trade all throughout Southeast Asia, the Philippines, and other nearby regions. However, as they were looking toward the south, incursions began to occur in their northern frontiers.

These incursions into the reaches of Manchuria were instigated by Russian adventurers seeking land and resources outside of Russia's own known boundaries. They ventured into lands whose exact boundaries had been obscure for centuries. These daring Russians decided to create their own definition of where the Russian border was by building fortresses in the region. This led to direct conflict between the Russian and Qing forces in 1685. Ultimately, the Russians signed the Treaty of Nerchinsk with China in 1689 to settle these border disputes.

When the Kangxi Emperor died in 1722, he was succeeded by his son and heir, who became known as the Yongzheng Emperor. His reign, which lasted until 1735, was much shorter and more troubled than that of his father. During his time on the throne, the Qing attempted to absorb many non-Han groups that had long lived on the periphery of Chinese society. They encouraged Han colonization of frontier regions, co-opted local tribal elites into official roles, and even enforced the Manchu queue hairstyle on Han men as a visible sign of submission. Still, bloody revolts, like the Miao uprisings, made it clear that these efforts were often ham-fisted and poorly received.

After his death in 1735, he was succeeded by a much more successful leader—the Qianlong Emperor. The Qianlong Emperor came to power with an already well-established and efficient bureaucratic system in place, as well as a treasury overflowing with resources. It was up to him to make the most of all this.

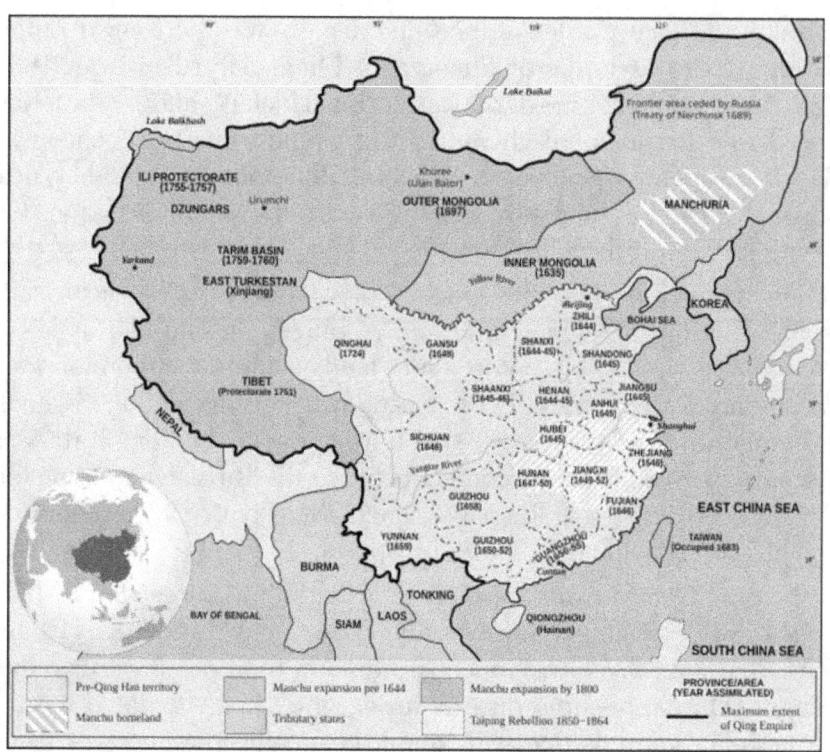

The Qing dynasty around 1820.[15]

The Qing began to allow some quiet outreach to foreign nations. Christian missionaries, in particular, had gained acceptance, with Qing officials viewing the religion as harmless and those who espoused it as peaceful and perhaps even helpful. However, when a dispute arose over ancestor worship among Chinese converts, the emperor began to change his mind. There was a great controversy between Christian missionaries over what it actually meant to revere one's ancestors. Some Christians allowed the traditional practice of ancestor worship, insisting that it was merely a cultural artifact of Chinese society and that it should not impact one's belief in Christianity at all. Others insisted that this form of worshipful reverence was an example of polytheism and came straight from the pits of hell.

The situation came to a head when Pope Clement XI weighed in on the matter and forbade the practice outright. These developments were viewed as rather troubling disturbances by Qing officials and led to a push against Christian missionaries.

This would not put a stop to European inroads in China, though; instead, it would just make Europeans switch gears. Instead of missionaries, the Qing dynasty would be inundated with European merchants wishing to enter into trade. The British, like other Europeans, traded with China exclusively through the East India Company at the port of Canton (modern-day Guangzhou). Under the Canton System, all foreign merchants were confined to this port and forced to conduct trade through licensed Chinese merchant guilds known as the Cohong. They were restricted in their movements, required to pay heavy fees, and dependent on Chinese intermediaries to handle their goods and barter for them.

One of the most prized goods was tea. The British had grown rather fond of tea, and its trade had proved to be a lucrative enterprise. But as much as the British were addicted to tea from China, the British sought to inflict an altogether more virulent addiction on the Chinese by shipping them an enormous amount of opium.

Starting in the 1780s, the British East India Company was operating in tandem with local opium dealers to bring the drug to China. With these secret dealings in the background, on July 25th, 1793, a British delegation led by Ambassador George Macartney famously landed in China to seek greater trade opportunities with the Qing dynasty. George Macartney gained an audience with the Qianlong Emperor and was initially under the impression that his delegation was being well received. But after a while, he came to understand that he was merely being humored and delayed. He realized that his entreaties were being ignored. In October, the Qianlong Emperor made his intentions clear on the subject.

He basically stated that although foreigners, like the British, desired to have unfettered trade with China, the Chinese themselves did not actually need it. On the contrary, the Qianlong Emperor insisted that China had everything it could possibly want within its own borders. Essentially, the emperor was making it seem that it was really the Chinese who were doing the British a favor by allowing trade with them. The British were more or less told that Canton would remain the port through which trade would be conducted and that the status quo of the situation would not change.

Little did the emperor know that the British had been quietly cultivating opium addiction in China. They indeed had something that many Chinese craved. After collecting opium crops in British-controlled India, the Brits brought shipments of the drug into Canton. An estimated four thousand chests of opium were delivered in 1787. This number steadily increased to an annual amount of some thirty thousand chests by the year 1833.

The Qianlong Emperor abdicated in 1796 in favor of his son, the Jiaqing Emperor, although he continued to wield influence until his death in 1799. The empire was grappling with rising opium addiction. The Jiaqing Emperor found it difficult to manage this growing crisis. He ruled until 1820, when he died of a stroke at the age of fifty-nine. His successor, the Daoguang Emperor, recognized the severity of the opium problem and appointed Lin Zexu as commissioner to combat it.[i]

During the course of Lin Zexu's investigation, he sent a letter to none other than Britain's monarch, Queen Victoria. In this missive to the young queen, who had just taken the throne a few years prior, the Chinese commissioner demanded to know why the British were so intent on shipping harmful narcotics into Chinese ports after China had been—as he described it—so gracious to them. There was a desire to know whether this was just blind greed on the part of British merchants or if there was a larger, more complicated geopolitical strategy at work. To this very day, there is much argument over what the British government was up to. Were they trying to use opium to put a dent in Chinese power?

After writing this letter, Lin Zexu began cracking down on the opium issue. In 1839, he began arresting addicts and dealers. At the beginning of his campaign, the commissioner arrested numerous addicts and local dealers and seized around seventy thousand opium pipes.

Lin Zexu also had a large team of assistants who took it upon themselves to destroy the opium itself, burning it up and dumping its remnants into the ocean. For the commissioner, it was a legal matter; these people were breaking the law by using and selling what the Chinese government considered to be an illegal drug. The recreational smoking of opium had been made illegal in 1729, although opium was allowed for some medicinal purposes. Even so, opium kept coming in by the boatload—literally. In fact, it is said that by the early 1800s, thousands of chests of opium were being shipped to China per year. This opium was shipped into China by foreign vessels that typically would not allow Chinese officials to inspect them. That began to change under the direction of Lin Zexu.[ii]

---

[i] Tanner, Harold. *China: A History From the Great Qing Empire through the People's Republic of China, 1644-2009.* 2010. Pg. 60.

[ii] Tanner, Harold. *China: A History From the Great Qing Empire through the People's Republic of China, 1644-2009.* Pg. 75.

However, when Commissioner Lin Zexu seized massive quantities of British opium in Canton and ordered it publicly destroyed, the British were outraged. Even though the opium was confiscated on Chinese soil, British officials claimed it was a direct assault on their national honor and, more importantly to them, on their profits. The saber-rattling began almost immediately. By November 1839, the First Opium War had officially kicked off, with naval skirmishes breaking out between British warships and Chinese junks near the Chinese coast.

The overall conflict between Britain and China was largely a naval one, with sea battles occurring up and down China's coastline. At one point, the British managed to make their way up the Yangtze River all the way to Nanjing (formerly known as Nanking). This conflict raged until the beaten and battered Chinese sued for peace in 1842.

The resulting peace treaty (the Treaty of Nanking) had the Chinese cough up several supposed treaty ports, with Guangzhou, Xiamen, Fuzhou, Ningbo, and Shanghai being among them. More importantly, the British had been given Hong Kong Island. The British would continue to add to their control of Hong Kong, which they ruled until 1997, when the British government formally ceded control of the city back to China.

Along with all of this, China was forced to pay a huge amount of money for damages. Chinese authorities also received a terrible blow since the treaty forced them to treat British visitors with extra special care. Due to the imposition of extraterritorial measures, any Brit suspected of committing a crime could not be handled by the Chinese justice system. Instead, they were to be placed into the hands of British authorities, who would then subject them to British law rather than Chinese law. This meant that if a visiting sailor harassed Chinese citizens, the best the Chinese government could do to protect its own people was to alert British authorities and hope that the British would deal fairly with the administration of justice.

It was indeed a humiliating thing for the Chinese not to be able to enforce their own laws when visiting foreigners chose to break them. The Chinese had attempted to use their own legal mechanisms to thwart the shipment of opium by foreigners. Now, they could not even detain a foreign opium smuggler even if they wanted to. Their hands were most certainly tied.

Another blow to Chinese esteem was that the British insisted that the Chinese give them "Most Favored Nation Status." This meant the British would take on a dominant role in any potential treaties China might make with other actors on the world stage. The situation would grow worse for China as other countries sought their own unequal treaty arrangements.

China was increasingly preyed upon. It was pushed around by foreign powers, and its ability to respond weakened by the year. The pressure finally tipped in 1856 when Qing officials boarded the *Arrow*, a Chinese-owned ship flying the British flag, suspecting piracy. The seizure infuriated the British, who saw it as a blatant affront to their rights and used it as justification for war.

Meanwhile, the Xianfeng Emperor, who had inherited an already collapsing empire in 1850, was losing his grip. While he remained emperor in name, much of the real power slipped from his hands, especially as regional armies and court regents began steering the state through the crisis. The Second Opium War erupted shortly afterward, and amid military defeats and rebellion, the emperor would die in 1861, not long after the court fled Beijing.[i]

During the Second Opium War, troops were sent inland. In December 1857, the British disembarked at Canton and marched all the way to the local governor's home. They seized the governor and sent him packing all the way to British-controlled India. Yes, even though the British insisted on a hands-off policy as it pertained to British citizens, the British brazenly kidnapped a Chinese governor and held him prisoner.

Worse was yet to come. In 1859, the British again sent troops into mainland China, and this time, they marched all the way to Beijing. Here, they set fire to the famed Summer Palace, burning it to the ground. The Chinese were in a state of shock and ultimately capitulated to demands. They signed a brand new treaty on October 24th, 1860.

---

[i] Tanner, Harold. *China: A History From the Great Qing Empire through the People's Republic of China, 1644-2009.* Pg. 87.

The Summer Palace.[16]

This treaty led to more territorial concessions from China, giving the British control of the Kowloon Peninsula. It also had China paying out more money in addition to the indemnities that were already being paid. China was forced to allow Christian missionaries to freely preach in China, something it had previously resisted. But even though Chinese officials were being forced to agree to such draconian terms, that did not mean the large population of China itself was going to agree and be on the same page.

Well before the treaty was inked, China was already convulsed by one of its deadliest upheavals in history: the Taiping Rebellion. This popular revolt had political and quasi-religious overtones. At the heart of this uprising was a local rebel leader (and a shaman of sorts) named Hong Xiuquan.

Hong came from a rather obscure background. As a young adult, he had failed the civil service exams and subsequently had a nervous breakdown. He then began to have visions (some might say hallucinations), in which he saw a man with a white beard, extolling him to pick up his sword and battle against the forces of darkness. He also saw a younger man, whom he believed to be the old man's son.

Initially, Hong did not understand what he was seeing, but after reading a Christian tract, he had an epiphany. He came to believe that the old man was God and that the young man was none other than God's only begotten son, Jesus Christ. This was not the end of Hong's revelations, though. He soon came to believe that he was also a son of God, making him Christ's own brother.

Hong pored over the scriptures and decided that he was picking up where Jesus had left off. Similar to how Jesus remarked that the "Kingdom of Heaven was at hand," Hong began to proclaim that he was destined to usher in this heavenly kingdom and that the heart of this kingdom would be located right inside China itself.

Hong had a lot of followers, especially among poor farmers and those who felt abandoned by the Qing government. But China—then as now—was vast and diverse, and not everyone was buying what Hong was selling. Faced with opposition and unwillingness to convert, Hong decided that persuasion alone was not going to cut it. He raised a massive rebel army, and in 1853, they stormed Nanjing, capturing it and declaring it the capital of their so-called Heavenly Kingdom. A couple of years later, in 1855, he and his forces laid siege to Beijing. The rebels were pushed back at this point, but the preoccupied Qing government was not able to stamp out the rebellion completely. The rebels holed up in their stronghold in Nanjing, where they continued to defy the Qing.

A scene of the Taiping Rebellion.[17]

In January 1864, the armies of the Qing managed to surround the bulk of the Taiping military in Nanjing. The Qing forces had their foes right where they wanted them, and they laid siege to the city. Hong perished in the struggle. His followers were likely disheartened after his death, which led to the fall of the city. By June, the Qing were in full control of the Kingdom of Heaven's capital.[i]

---

[i] Tanner, Harold. *China: A History From the Great Qing Empire through the People's Republic of China, 1644-2009.* Pg. 88.

Although the Qing defeated the rebels, the fact that they had held out for so long showed just how difficult a time the Qing were having. They faced multiple outside threats and internal discord, so they had to put out many fires on different fronts.

There were still problems to deal with, especially when a resurgent Japan came to take its piece of the Chinese pie. Japan had watched very closely what was happening in China, and its people were determined not to have it replicated in Japanese territory.

In 1868, in an effort to rapidly modernize, Japan kicked off the Meiji Restoration, which was named after the ambitious Japanese Emperor Meiji. While China had failed to modernize due to the lack of an industrial base and isolationist policies, Japan was astonishingly successful in its efforts. In a feverish rush of activity akin to the Manhattan Project or the moon landing, Japan pulled all of its resources and manpower into a tremendous national effort. The country managed to make rapid advancements that would have taken other countries decades (if not centuries) in just a few years.

Japan developed a strong industrial base and began pumping out modern armaments. These armaments were sent aboard brand-new Japanese naval craft, allowing the military to begin to make inroads against the staggering and failing power of China. This aggressive posturing came to a head in 1894 when Japan invaded Korea.

This was not the first time Japan had tried its luck at invading Korea. You may recall that Japan had launched an invasion of Korea during the Ming dynasty. It took a considerable amount of resources to push the Japanese out, and it is believed the invasion contributed to the weakening of the Ming dynasty, eventually allowing the Manchu to take over and establish the Qing dynasty. Yes, the Ming had repelled the Japanese at great cost, but the Qing would not be so lucky.

This second historic invasion of Korea by Japan was a clear bit of aggression on Japan's part, but it was not merely motivated by conquest (although that was certainly a part of it). Many Japanese military advisers viewed the taking of Korea as a preemptive defensive measure to better safeguard Japan itself. At its closest point, Korea lies just 120 miles from Japan. The Japanese feared that if China fell to the Europeans, Korea would soon be occupied by them as well. If Korea had become a European colony, it would not have been too hard to launch an invasion from Korea against Japan. The Japanese basically reasoned that if China could not protect Korea, then they would go in and take control of it for themselves.

When the Korean government was threatened by an internal coup attempt, it asked the Chinese for military assistance. However, the Japanese inserted themselves into the picture. It was not long before Japanese and Chinese troops came to blows. The fighting over Korea, which ultimately became known as the First Sino-Japanese War, erupted in July 1894.

During this conflict, the Japanese, despite their much smaller numbers, managed to deal China stunning defeats in battle after battle. The Japanese demonstrated that they had a much keener grasp of advanced military equipment and methods. In an incredible reversal, mighty China actually had to bow down to Japan. In the subsequent treaty China made with the victor, the Chinese agreed to give up Taiwan and relinquish all claims on Korea. Japan would slowly sink its teeth into Korea, first proclaiming it as a Japanese protectorate before annexing the territory completely in 1910.

China's embarrassing defeat in the First Sino-Japanese War sparked a wave of resentment and unrest among the Chinese masses. That bitterness simmered for years until it boiled over in 1900. In northern China, the martial societies known as the "Boxers" rose in a violent campaign against missionaries, foreign legations, and the Qing's foreign entanglements.

Similar to the Taiping Rebellion, the Boxer Rebellion was a revolt with religious overtones. The Boxers were called as such because they were martial artists who knew how to use their fists. This skill was apparently on full display when they made their way into Beijing in 1900 and began randomly assaulting the foreigners they found there.

The Boxers seem to have especially had it out for foreign missionaries. They feared that the foreign missionaries were spies and saw them as instigators. The Boxers also resented the fact that they would often intervene in legal matters between Christian Chinese and non-Christian Chinese residents.[i]

As a massive horde of angry ruffians descended upon them in Beijing, foreigners were forced to seek refuge in and around foreign embassies. Chinese Christians were also forced to flee, as their churches were burned

---

[i] Tanner, Harold. *China: A History From the Great Qing Empire through the People's Republic of China, 1644-2009*. Pg. 97.

and people were assaulted. It is believed that thousands of Chinese Christians were forced to leave to avoid the violence of the Boxers.

This tumult certainly did not go unnoticed. It soon got the attention of foreign power brokers and a coalition of European states, as well as Japan. A multinational force, said to have been around twenty thousand strong, was sent in to put down the revolt.

Even though the Chinese government claimed the uprising was spontaneous in nature, the current Qing ruler, Empress Dowager Cixi, was still held accountable. Upon the threat of further military intervention, she was forced to sign the Boxer Protocol. Under these stipulations, China was forced to allow the stationing of foreign troops in Beijing and was forced to pay a hefty fee in reparations. Furthermore, any Chinese organization deemed to have even a hint of anti-foreigner sentiment was officially banned under penalty of execution. In doing so, Empress Dowager Cixi signed what could be called a death warrant for both her regime and herself. The crushing terms of the Boxer Protocol stripped the Qing of what little autonomy it had left, and the dynasty was never the same again. She died on November 15th, 1908, officially from dysentery—or perhaps a complication of pneumonia—but rumors of foul play lingered for decades.

However, if outside powers thought that coming down hard on the Qing dynasty would bring order to China, they were gravely mistaken. This latest crackdown only led to even more discontent among the Chinese.

Up until this point, many of the rebellions that broke out were supposedly done in the name of the Qing. The Boxers claimed they were trying to restore China's prestige on behalf of the Qing dynasty, which was why their attacks were on foreigners, not on Qing officials. According to scholar and historian Jonathan Clements, the slogan shouted by the Boxers was "Support the Qing, expel the foreigners."[i]

In the aftermath of the failed Boxer uprising, the rebels seemed to have a change of heart. It was realized that the only way to bring China back to its glory days was to topple the Qing government itself. From this point forward, the attacks were not so much on outsiders as they were on Qing insiders.

Around this time, a young Chinese woman named Qiu Jin came to

---

[i] Clements, Jonathan. *A Brief History of China*. Pg. 330.

prominence. Born in 1875, Qiu Jin came of age during the Boxer Rebellion. She went on to marry and have two children, but the traditional life of a Chinese housewife just did not satisfy her. She wanted more. Qui Jin ended up leaving her husband and children (something highly unusual for the time) and traveling to Japan, where she studied abroad.

Befriending local intelligentsia, she learned about philosophy and all manner of political and social theories. She then returned to China in 1905 and became actively involved in anti-Qing revolts. Along with being a rabble-rouser, Qui Jin was known as a great writer. She could stir even the hardest of hearts with her stirring poetic prose. Many of her poems and other writings could be found in a magazine-style periodical, for which she served as the editor.

Qui Jin was not only a champion of overthrowing the Qing dynasty; she was also an advocate for women's rights. She condemned the practice of foot binding, which was still widespread. Foot binding is the practice of binding up the feet of Chinese girls so that their feet will be small. However, their feet would also be deformed as a result.

Qiu Jin drew a direct parallel between the practice of foot binding and the constant social binding of women. Even though foot binding was an obvious means of physically crippling Chinese women so they could obtain "desirable" feet, the oppressive, male-dominated Chinese society had other methods at its disposal to keep women confined. Girls were routinely denied an education; they were kept deliberately illiterate so they would not get any ideas about independence. Most women were forced into arranged marriages and treated as bargaining chips in family deals, with no say in the matter. Once married, they had little to no legal rights. They were unable to own property, initiate divorce, or move freely. Their lives were expected to play out in the shadows, behind doors, and far from the public eye. Even in widowhood, they were chained to outdated ideals. They were expected to remain chaste for the rest of their lives, even if it meant a lifetime alone. In Qiu Jin's eyes, all of this was just another kind of binding—and she was determined to cut the cords.

Qui Jin was most certainly a progressive for the period, and she believed that obtaining full and equal rights for all Chinese was the only possible path forward. She was known for her eccentric (at least eccentric by early 1900s standards) habit of dressing like a man, not wearing makeup, and riding around on a horse, with a Japanese sword dangling at her side. She definitely stood out from the crowd and was rather hard to miss. But she also never made any attempt to hide.

Along with being a writer and editor, she also ran a girls' school called the Datong School for Girls. However, the school also served as a front for the instruction of Chinese republican radicals who were hellbent on overthrowing the Qing government and installing a Chinese republic in its place. Once these activities were uncovered, the heavy hand of the Qing came down on the Datong School and ultimately Qui Jin herself. She could hardly deny being involved since she was nursing a badly hurt hand when the authorities arrived. She had been injured in a failed attempt to make a bomb. Her own cousin had also been recently implicated in an attack on the police.

Her friends had received word of the crackdown ahead of time and tried to warn Qui to flee. Qui Jin was adamant in her refusal to do so. She insisted that instead of running from the Qing officials she had been harrying, she was going to stand her ground. It is unclear what she hoped to achieve besides becoming a martyr for the cause, but she insisted that she would stay.

Qui Jin stayed inside while soldiers surrounded the compound and engaged in gunfights with the students and rebels outside. The troops then went in and grabbed Qui Jin, dragging her out into the street. She was then brought to the local station, where she was brutally interrogated. She refused to confess to any crimes, so a confession was written for her. Her torturers then asked her to sign it. She refused. Supposedly, she wrote the words to one last poem instead. She was then sentenced to death.

She was convicted without a trial and without a jury. The sentence was carried out a short time later. In 1907, Qui Jin had her head chopped off in a public square known as Xuanting Crossing. She became a martyr for the revolution. She did not live to see the events play out, but it all happened in rather rapid-fire fashion after her death. In the following year, 1908, Empress Dowager Cixi perished. She left the throne to her two-year-old nephew, who became the Xuantong Emperor.

Of course, the infant would have advisers rule in his stead, but despite any best intentions, a renewed reign of Qing authority was simply not to be. In 1911,

A colorized photograph of Sun Yat-sen.[18]

the Qing dynasty collapsed under its own ineffectual weight. Many rebel factions had made this collapse possible, but a radical revolutionary by the name of Sun Yat-sen had risen to particular prominence.

Sun Yat-sen had trained as a physician in his youth and often applied his diagnostic instincts to the deeper ailments of Chinese society. He concluded that it was the outdated thinking and oppressive structures of the monarchy that were poisoning the body politic. Driven by that insight, he became a radical revolutionary determined to overthrow the Qing dynasty.

His zeal got him into serious trouble. Forced into exile, Sun Yat-sen ended up in London. In October 1896, he was detained at the Chinese legation for over a week. The legation attempted to send him back to Beijing for execution, but thanks to the intervention of sympathetic British allies and mounting public outcry, Sun was released. The incident gave him international fame and further legitimacy as a revolutionary leader.[i]

Back in China, the Qing monarchy was on its last legs. The Guangxu Emperor, who had once shown promise as a reformer, died under mysterious circumstances while under house arrest. Empress Dowager Cixi, who was still the power behind the throne, named her infant nephew Puyi as emperor. But with Puyi too young to rule, power passed to a series of ineffective regents. Within just a few years, the entire imperial system collapsed. In 1912, Puyi abdicated, bringing more than two thousand years of dynastic rule in China to an end.[ii]

Yuan Shikai.[19]

Although Sun Yat-sen was a big player in all of this, he ultimately deferred authority to Yuan Shikai, a fellow revolutionary and former military general. Sun Yat-sen saw to it that Yuan became the provisional president for what he hoped would be a Chinese republic. However, Yuan became a bit power-mad, and in 1915, he actually tried to

---

[i] Tanner, Harold. *China: A History From the Great Qing Empire through the People's Republic of China, 1644-2009.* Pg. 96.

[ii] Tanner, Harold. *China: A History From the Great Qing Empire through the People's Republic of China, 1644-2009.* Pg. 117.

make himself emperor for life.

The other factions within the movement quickly turned against Yuan when they found out, and they pulled the plug on his ambitious pretensions. Yuan's attempt was thwarted, but China was thrown into chaos once again, with various factions fighting each other.

The world was changing in the meantime. World War I had erupted, and in the midst of all that, a massive communist revolution erupted in Russia in 1917, laying the foundations for the Soviet Union. This ideology quickly spread to China, and in 1921, China's Communist Party first took shape.

Sun Yat-sen passed his authority to a powerful general named Chiang Kai-shek, who was able to gain dominance over the other warring factions of the revolution. By 1929, Chiang Kai-shek seemingly had a solid grip on the country, as well as a powerful base in the capital city of Nanjing (Nanking).

However, the Communists were growing underground and out of sight under the leadership of Mao Zedong. Mao Zedong began his career as a young radical and steadily rose through the ranks. The Communists would emerge in force in 1931 after a Chinese Soviet Republic was declared. This base lasted for a few years before it was dismantled by Chiang Kai-shek and his Nationalist army.

Mao Zedong—whatever his faults—was a shrewd and cunning military strategist. He knew that the Communists were not yet ready to face the might of the Nationalist army head-on. So, instead, he perfected a form of highly effective guerrilla warfare. He and his army hid just out of reach of the Nationalists. He directed his forces to only engage in quick surgical strikes against specific targets before melting back into the wilderness. This strategy whittled down the fighting capacity of the Nationalists, and the Communists were able to minimize their losses.

The struggle between these two camps would be interrupted and effectively put on hold when Japan once again made aggressive inroads in China. The Japanese, who had already seized Korea, decided to seize the neighboring region of northeastern China, otherwise known as Manchuria. The Japanese engineered a regime change by installing Manchu leadership and branding the puppet state of Manchukuo as a newly resurrected Manchu realm. They installed the exiled former emperor Puyi as ruler in a political move meant to legitimize their control. The audacity of creating a revived monarchy under Japanese direction alarmed both the

Nationalists and the Communists. In the face of this foreign imposition, they agreed to a fragile, temporary truce. They put aside their civil war and united, at least in name, to resist Japanese aggression.

Chapter 7: World War II and China's Civil War

"The superior man, when resting in safety, does not forget that danger may come."

-Confucius[i]

China's renewed problems with Japan first erupted in 1931 during the Mukden incident. The Mukden incident occurred in the Japanese-controlled region of Manchuria. Although the incident is still shrouded in some obscurity, most scholars believe the Japanese sabotaged their own railroad tracks and then turned around and blamed the Chinese for it.

The Japanese used this as a reason to forcibly occupy the region and ultimately transform it into a Japanese-controlled puppet state, which they referred to as Manchukuo. The Japanese were creeping steadily closer to the Chinese heartland, as they now controlled Korea and the bordering region of Manchuria. From 1932 to 1935, they would seize more territory in Inner Mongolia and make aggressive advances toward the Shanxi, Shandong, and Suiyuan regions.

Chiang Kai-shek's Nationalist government mostly ignored this aggression, feeling as if the bigger threat to Chinese society was the Communists inside China. Mao Zedong and his band were forced into hiding. They embarked upon the "Long March" into the remote reaches

---

[i] Brewer, D. *Quotes of Confucius and Their Interpretations: A Words of Wisdom Collection Book.* Pg. 45.

of China from October 1934 to October 1935. This retreat from Chiang Kai-shek's Nationalist troops would have the Communists trekking some six thousand miles. They marched from Jiangxi, located in China's southeast, all the way to Shaanxi province in the north.[i]

This sentiment would change on July 7th, 1937. Ever since the Boxer Protocol, China had been forced to allow nations, including Japan, which had legates in Beijing, to have their own military guard to serve as protection. This was due to the fact that the Boxers had attacked foreigners, and the Chinese government had seemed unable or unwilling to protect them. It was for this reason that the Japanese had troops on the Marco Polo Bridge in the first place.

The Marco Polo Bridge incident occurred when a Japanese soldier did not return to his post. The Japanese insisted on being able to send in troops to look for the missing man. The Chinese refused, which led to a tense stand-off that ultimately resulted in the exchange of gunfire. This incident spiraled into the Second Sino-Japanese War. Just a couple of years later, this war would become a theater of conflict in the larger conflagration of World War II. In fact, the Marco Polo Bridge incident could be considered the starting point of World War II, although historians generally cite Germany's 1939 invasion of Poland as the start of the war.

In 1940, Japan entered into an alliance with fellow fascist belligerents, Germany and Italy. They would battle the Allied forces, which were led by the United States, Britain, the Soviet Union, and, ultimately, China.

After the Marco Polo Bridge incident, the fighting continued to escalate. By December of 1937, Japanese troops were storming into Nanjing, which led to the infamous "Rape of Nanking." It is believed that the Japanese killed hundreds of thousands of Chinese, many of them civilians.

The use of the word "rape" is not an exaggeration either since the Japanese routinely used rape as a weapon of war and retribution. The city of Nanjing saw some of the worst depredations in recorded history. Japanese troops stormed into homes. They murdered husbands, fathers, and sons, and then they had their way with the women living there.

---

[i] Tanner, Harold. *China: A History From the Great Qing Empire through the People's Republic of China, 1644-2009*. Pg. 163.

Captured Chinese captives. It is believed that all of them were killed within days.[30]

Before the year 1937 was through, Nanjing had been decimated, and other major Chinese cities had likewise fallen in quick succession. Shanghai fell to the Japanese, as did Guangzhou. The Japanese ended up dominating northern China and set up their own capital in Nanjing. The Chinese government was forced to move farther south and regroup in Sichuan province.

Despite suffering devastating losses, the Chinese army was still intact and could tap a large pool of manpower. Although Sichuan province had its fair share of resources, China's main industrial capacity was in the northeastern cities that Japan had taken over. The Chinese forces had also lost access to important ports that were crucial for the importation of war materiel.

Even so, the Chinese resistance refused to give up and would remain a stubborn thorn in Japan's side. This led to even more brutal tactics. The Japanese air force began a ruthless bombing campaign, hoping to shock the Chinese resistance into submission. The Japanese also tried their hand at propaganda to bring the Chinese populace on their side.

In 1940, the Japanese took things a step further by installing a puppet ruler, Wang Jingwei, a former political rival of Chiang Kai-shek who had turned collaborator. Stationed in Nanjing, Wang led what was called the Reorganized National Government of China. While this move gave the appearance of legitimacy, it was widely dismissed across China. The memories of Japanese atrocities, particularly the horrors of Nanjing, were still fresh. Even those who might have once sympathized with Wang were unlikely to lend him their support under such circumstances.

Demonstrating a strong sense of patriotism (whether they supported the Communist or Nationalist factions), the Chinese citizens rose up in solidarity against the Japanese. Japanese-controlled areas became depopulated as Chinese fled south and west to more distant reaches where they would be free from the grasp of their aggressors. These Chinese refugees joined the armed struggle or provided much-needed manpower to build up infrastructure in the new bases of resistance.

Although the Nationalists and the Communists were ostensibly working together to push back the Japanese, Chiang Kai-shek and Mao Zedong quietly consolidated their own bases of power, preparing for an inevitable new round of fighting between them as soon as the Japanese were defeated.

During the war, Chiang Kai-shek, as leader of the Nationalists, was the public face of China. He was the officially recognized leader of the Chinese, and the Allied powers dealt with him. Mao Zedong was an underground leader during this period. It is likely no one ever dreamed that he would eventually rise up to become China's supreme leader.

By 1942, the Japanese were already in retreat. Japan had made the mistake of bombing Pearl Harbor, Hawaii, which brought the United States into the war. After the Battle of Midway, which took place in early June 1942, Japan was steadily being pushed back on all fronts. The Japanese were ultimately defeated in the summer of 1945.

Mao Zedong had been consolidating his grip on the CCP (the Chinese Communist Party). Shortly after the war had come to a close, a referendum was held in which Mao was made chairman of the party. Right on the heels of Mao being made chairman, Chiang Kai-shek extended an invitation to Mao to speak with him.

Mao met Chiang at the Nationalist stronghold in Chongqing in Sichuan province. The meeting received worldwide attention, with the international press widely covering the event. The two men seemed to be in good spirits as they drank and spoke with one another. They likely had a lot to reminisce about, whether they were swapping war stories about the Japanese or even accounts of run-ins that their mutual armed forces had with each other.

The most encouraging thing for witnesses to the talks was simply the fact that these two were *talking*. For one brief moment, it seemed that perhaps the two factions of China could come together and that some sort of compromise might be made in order to avoid civil war. However, such things were not meant to be. Despite the nice talk the two had with each other, it was only a short time later that the previously stalled conflict between the Nationalists and the Communists reignited.

It was a long, bitter struggle, but the Communists eventually gained the upper hand. The Nationalists were ultimately pushed right off the mainland of China and forced to evacuate to the island of Taiwan. The Japanese, who had previously controlled Taiwan, had already left, leaving a power vacuum in their absence.

China entered the postwar era deeply unsettled but with a flicker of promise. The Cairo Declaration of November 1943 committed the Allies to restore both Taiwan and Manchuria to Chinese control, specifically to the Nationalist Republic of China under Chiang Kai-shek, not Mao's Communists. This guarantee still fuels today's Taiwan question.

After Japan's surrender, Chiang was designated China's postwar leader, but Beijing's recognition could not translate into instant control. In Manchuria, as Japanese forces withdrew, Communist troops under Lin Biao and Zhu De surged northward, seizing Soviet-captured armaments, recruiting former Manchukuo soldiers, and establishing bases in rail-hub and industrial zones. They even disrupted arrival routes for Nationalist reinforcements by destroying rail lines and controlling key ports.

By late 1945, Chiang's forces—though recognized internationally—had only advanced to Mukden (today's Shenyang) and parts of southern China. Meanwhile, the Communists dominated much of the northeast and sizable territories across northern China. The country was effectively carved into two competing spheres: the Communist-held north and the Nationalist south.

A split as deep as this could easily have become permanent; just look at North and South Korea or Vietnam. Yet history ran a different course. As the civil war resumed and the Communists steadily advanced, the Nationalists faltered. By 1949, Chiang and his followers were driven off the mainland, fleeing to Taiwan. Mao proclaimed the People's Republic of China, while Taiwan continued under the Republic of China, a status the island maintains to this day.

It took just a few years after Japan's surrender in 1945 for the Communist faction in China to triumph over the Nationalists. From the fall of the Qing dynasty through Japanese invasion and the subsequent civil war, China had been through quite a bit. However, China's struggle for survival and identity was far from over.

Chapter 8: Red China Rising

"For many years, we Communists have struggled for a cultural revolution as well as for a political and economic revolution, and our aim is to build a new society and a new state for the Chinese nation. That new society and new state will have not only a new politics and a new economy but a new culture."

-Mao Zedong[i]

The communist People's Republic of China was declared on the mainland on October 1st, 1949. The communist Chinese turned inward to figure out just what kind of government and society they were going to form.

Mao and his comrades had some rather lofty ideals that they wanted to fulfill. They wanted to absolutely transform the lives of the average Chinese citizen. They also wanted to fulfill many of the same ambitions that those who rebelled against the Qing in the early 1900s had sought. They wanted a strong, independent nation that was not beholden to the interests of outside forces. They wanted to establish a nation that they could all be proud of, one that would not be kicked around by outside nations. Mao and his followers also wanted to become a wealthy country that had respect on the world stage and a strong army. These were essentially the same ambitions of the very Nationalists the Communists had defeated. However, the Nationalists and Communists differed significantly in how society should be run. The Nationalists sought

---

[i] Clements, Jonathan. *A Brief History of China.* Pg. 348.

democratic freedom (even though it was not always implemented in the early days) for the average person, while the Communists were steadfast in their Marxist ideology, which called for government controls on just about every aspect of Chinese life.

After seizing control of mainland China in 1949, the Communist leadership found itself in uncharted waters. Most of its senior figures had been guerrilla fighters, not administrators, and running one of the world's largest nations was a different kind of battle. Their first priority was the countryside—the heartland of their revolution. They pushed through sweeping land reforms, broke up the holdings of wealthy landlords, and redistributed them to the peasants who had long backed the Communist cause.

Once their grip on power was secure, the focus shifted. By the mid-1950s, Beijing began looking beyond the rice paddies and toward the cities. Industrial growth, centralized planning, and urban infrastructure now became the priorities. This transition was not without friction since policies designed for rural China often clashed with the realities of urban life, but it marked the beginning of the state's long push to modernize China's cities as well as its countryside.

Mao Zedong, in the meantime, began to speak of his desire to create a solid socialist enclave within China and then project that ideology onto the world stage. According to Communists, this meant that cities needed to stop being consumers of goods and become producers of goods. In this struggle for production dominance, he advised that there would have to be a class struggle in order to bring these aims to fruition. The leadership of China would be a dictatorship, but it would be a *people's dictatorship*. The average citizen might not have fully understood all of these new terms. They were weary of decades of war. Most Chinese simply wanted a return to some sort of civilized society. As such, many complied and did their best to follow the communist state's new decrees. Communist-backed police and military units were created and helped greatly in the establishment of order, especially as it pertained to putting a stop to roving bandits, which had become prevalent due to the previous chaos.

China was trying to turn inward at this stage in its development so that it could focus on rebuilding and restructuring its society. But no matter how much China desired to turn its attention to internal affairs, the world stage would soon come calling again in the form of the Korean War.

In the summer of 1950, communist forces from North Korea stormed across the 38th parallel into South Korea. After gaining authorization from the United Nations to intervene, the United States led the charge to drive the North Koreans back. The Soviet Union came out in support of North Korea, as did China.

The Chinese would become directly involved in the war by secretly (at least at first) deploying their own troops into North Korea to take on the American, South Korean, and other allied fighters. An estimated 250,000 Chinese troops were sent to fight alongside the North Koreans. The war was a bloody one, but the United States and its allies managed to push the North Koreans back.

Ultimately, the war ended in an armistice in July 1953. The boundary between North and South Korea was once again the 38th parallel, and the area was established as a demilitarized zone (DMZ). Yes, after all of that bloodshed, the participants in this carnage were right back where they had started.

Right around the time of the Korean War, China also intervened in Tibet. China had long considered Tibet its own territory despite Tibet's history of independence. Tibet had enjoyed de facto independence ever since the fall of the Qing dynasty, but after the Communists consolidated their power in 1949, they started to look toward reestablishing Chinese authority over the Tibetans.

The Chinese launched an invasion of Tibet in 1950. Interestingly, although China's actions were considered an invasion from an outside perspective, the Chinese have always referred to this incident as the peaceful liberation of Tibet. Perspective, of course, is everything, but when Chinese troops came crashing across Tibet's borders on October 7th, 1950, the local Tibetans likely did not see anything all that peaceful or liberating about it. The world was quite distracted by the Korean War at the time, so very little attention was paid to what China was doing in Tibet.

Besides the forced takeover of Tibetan land, the most significant consequence of this action was the displacement of Tibet's religious and political leader, the Dalai Lama. After China's takeover of Tibet, the Dalai Lama was eventually driven into exile. He is still in exile to this day.

Tibet might have been forced to toe the Communist line, but Mao Zedong did not always present himself as an unbending autocrat. In 1956, he launched what became known as the Hundred Flowers Campaign, urging citizens to "let a hundred flowers bloom, let a hundred schools of thought contend." It was billed as an invitation for open debate, where intellectuals, workers, and officials alike could voice their concerns about the state and its leadership. For a brief moment, criticisms poured in.

By mid-1957, the mood changed abruptly. Mao declared that those outspoken critics were "rightists" seeking to undermine socialism. The campaign gave way to the Anti-Rightist Movement, and thousands of those who had spoken up were purged from their jobs, sent to labor camps, or imprisoned. Whether Mao had planned this reversal from the start or simply decided to turn the campaign into a purge once the criticism cut too deep remains debated, but the result was the same.

In 1958, Mao Zedong embarked upon his Great Leap Forward. This was an ambitious but ill-fated plan to rapidly speed up the industrialization of China. Mao sought to utilize the massive manpower available in China so he could bypass the need for heavy infrastructure.

Mao tried to mitigate the lack of large industrial factories by establishing backyard steel furnaces in local villages. Making matters worse, the technicians tapped to run these clumsy, improvised furnaces were often selected not for their merit or actual skill set and ability to forge steel but because of their adherence to communist ideology. Needless to say, the steel forged by these backyard furnaces was of horrendous quality. Even worse, orders were issued to strip all existing infrastructure of as much steel as possible so that it could be melted into more useful things.

All this accomplished was the destruction of much of China's usable steel. Good-quality tools, machinery, and structural supports were hauled off to be melted in crude backyard furnaces, only to emerge as brittle, worthless lumps of pig iron. These makeshift foundries devoured vast amounts of coal and lumber—the very fuels needed for industry and daily life—just to keep their fires burning.

Along with ineffective (and bizarre) attempts to industrialize China, the Great Leap Forward also sponsored agricultural reform. This also led to disaster. Collective farms were created, and strict quotas were established. It soon became common practice to lie about crop yields just to get a pat on the back from the Communist taskmasters. This led the government to think that they were achieving a bountiful harvest when the yields were actually quite dismal.

Matters became even worse. Mao Zedong, convinced that sparrows were harming grain production, ordered a nationwide campaign to eradicate them. As anyone with a basic grasp of ecosystems could have predicted, this was an ecological catastrophe in the making. Once the sparrow population plummeted, the insects they once kept in check, especially grain-devouring locusts, multiplied in swarms. With no natural predators left to control them, the locusts descended on fields across China, stripping crops bare. This, combined with other agricultural missteps of the Great Leap Forward, helped trigger a famine that raged until 1961.

A moratorium was finally placed on the Great Leap Forward the following year, in 1962. Ultimately, the Great Leap Forward can be summarized as a massive amount of investment, time, and energy that yielded very little. In fact, it did much more damage than it did any good.

This was not only evidenced by the starving and dying people of China but also by economic figures. Rather than propel China forward, the Great Leap Forward, which lasted from 1958 to 1962, saw the Chinese economy shrink.

Interestingly, although the funds were drying up, China still pulled together enough resources to establish itself as a nuclear power. In 1964, in the remote desert of Lop Nur, the Chinese successfully detonated their first atomic bomb—an achievement that shocked the rest of the world. It was codenamed Project 596, and it made China the fifth country on the planet with nuclear capability. Even more remarkable was that they had done it largely on their own. The Soviets had pulled out their scientists and blueprints in the late 1950s during the Sino-Soviet split. For Mao, the test was proof that China could stand shoulder to shoulder with the world's great powers, even though the country was still reeling from economic hardship.

And they weren't done yet. Less than three years later, in 1967, China stunned observers again by testing its first hydrogen bomb, leaping from atomic to thermonuclear status in record time. For a nation still struggling to feed itself, the message was unmistakable: China might be poor, but it was not to be underestimated.

Nevertheless, it was clear that something was deeply wrong with the communist system, China's leadership, or both. Tension and suspicion hung in the air. Out of this volatile climate came what would be called the Cultural Revolution. This was an all-out campaign to root out anyone deemed disloyal to communist ideals. It was nothing short of a reign of terror. The Cultural Revolution was driven by Mao Zedong's infamous Red Guards, who took it upon themselves to expose, humiliate, and often destroy perceived enemies of the revolution.

The Red Guards were a radical mass movement made up largely of indoctrinated youth. Mao understood that young people, with their impulsive energy and uncompromising idealism, were far more likely to throw themselves into the revolution with ferocity. They became his shock troops, carrying out vicious campaigns against anyone suspected of straying from the state's rigid communist orthodoxy.

This led to terrible scenes of students denouncing teachers, children denouncing parents, tenants evicting landlords, and random people on the street having the Red Guards haul them in for questioning. In particular, the Red Guards were seeking out those who were guilty of indulging in what was referred to as the Four Olds: old thinking, old culture, old customs, and old habits.

Mao Zedong's Cultural Revolution felt like it only came to an end when Red Guards overran much of Beijing, storming into the Forbidden City's backyard, only to be checked by armed resistance at the gates. But that was not the end of the chaos. By early 1968, the People's Liberation Army (the army of the People's Republic of China) was forcibly suppressing wild Red Guard factions across major urban centers. Later that year, Mao issued the order that sent most young radicals off to remote farms and rural provinces to be reeducated—a strategy that allowed the state to regain control.

The human cost was staggering. The estimates of those killed during the period range from one to two million, with some accounts suggesting even higher figures. Tens of millions more were persecuted, exiled, or displaced, including the sweeping Down to the Countryside Movement, which uprooted more than ten million urban youth. Entire families were torn apart. Intellectuals, suspected capitalists, and "class enemies" were purged in brutal mass campaigns.

Some of the worst atrocities occurred during mass killings and massacres, such as in Dao County, where over 7,600 were killed or forced to take their own lives. In 1970, the Chinese Communist Party even launched what was called the "One Strike-Three Antis Campaign," targeting supposed counterrevolutionaries, profiteers, and corrupt officials. Nearly 1.9 million people were labeled enemies, with hundreds of thousands arrested or executed, all in the name of ideological cleansing. This horror only truly wound down with Mao's death in 1976 and the arrest of the Gang of Four.

In many ways, the Cultural Revolution could be seen as Mao creating internal enemies for frustrated citizens to attack. This served as a release valve so they could vent their frustration. He likely figured it was better for them to vent their frustration on each other than to turn their wrath on him and his own failed policies.

In the meantime, China was going through external changes as well. Most notably, in July 1971, entreaties were made to the United States by way of President Richard Nixon's adviser, Henry Kissinger, and Mao's top fixer, Zhou Enlai. These two arranged for Nixon and Mao to meet with each other in the spring of 1972. The visit was a political coup for both Nixon and Mao and resulted in one of the most thought-provoking moments of the Cold War.

By this point, the Chinese had experienced a falling-out of sorts with their old benefactor, the Soviet Union. To describe it as a "falling-out" is putting it rather mildly, considering that border skirmishes had actually erupted between the two in 1969.

Mao had begun to fear the Soviet Union more than he ever admired it. He had watched with alarm during the Soviet invasion and occupation of Czechoslovakia in 1968. Czechoslovakia was already a communist, Soviet-aligned state, yet due to discord and internal division, the Soviets decided it was their business to forcibly intervene. This was part of the Brezhnev Doctrine (named after Soviet Premier Leonid Brezhnev), which stipulated that the Soviet Union could stage military interventions in fellow communist states if deemed necessary.

Considering the discord of the Cultural Revolution, Mao likely wondered if the Soviets were considering staging such an intervention in China. In consideration of all of this, Mao sought to distance himself from Soviet Russia and pull closer to the United States. Mao and Nixon shocked the world by forging a strong partnership with each other.

US President Richard Nixon meeting with Chairman Mao Zedong.[31]

Yes, China was communist, and America was capitalist, but these two found common ground with one another all the same. One major issue on Nixon's mind at this time was the Vietnam War. The war had been raging long before he became president and had been escalated primarily by his predecessor, President Lyndon Johnson. The war needed to come to an end, and Nixon wanted to be the president to conclude the conflict. Nixon and his advisers believed that China might hold the key to doing just that. The meeting had a lot on the table for the two to talk about, but the chance that China could weigh in and get the communist North Vietnamese to listen to reason was a big part of it. China was hoping to gain a bargaining chip against the Soviet Union, thereby increasing China's options and limiting dependence on the Soviets.

In 1972, shortly before Nixon's historic visit, Mao Zedong suffered a serious stroke that left him in declining health. Premier Zhou Enlai, already burdened with his own ailments, would be diagnosed two years later with terminal cancer. Both men knew their time was limited and began quietly considering who might carry the torch of leadership after them.

Both Mao and Zhou began pulling strings behind the scenes to try to bring their protégé, Deng Xiaoping, to prominence. This created a problem for Mao's wife, Jiang Qing, who was a big supporter of the

Cultural Revolution. Her own radicals had previously denounced Deng during the purges for advocating certain economic reforms. They declared that he had deviated from Marxist doctrine. She and her most vocal supporters, who were later referred to as the Gang of Four, came out in direct opposition to Mao and Zhou's choice for a successor.

This created a schism in the Chinese government and society, leading to just the kind of power struggle that most people wanted to avoid. When the economy began to buckle and Chinese prosperity diminished, the winds began to shift back in favor of Deng. The Cultural Revolution was very unpopular by this point, as were Jiang and the Gang of Four. China was seemingly now ready to hear more of what Deng had to say.

In late 1975, as Zhou Enlai was stricken by illness, Deng Xiaoping was quietly elevated, taking charge of key state functions. But when Zhou died, the political tides turned sharply. The Gang of Four, which still wielded power, targeted Deng for his "capitalist deviations," and he was purged—just as his economic reforms were starting to gain traction. Only after Mao died and the radicals were swept aside did Deng's ideas finally begin to win out.

After Mao Zedong died at the age of eighty-two in 1976, the Chinese finally turned against Mao's wife Jiang and the Gang of Four. They were all put on trial. Jiang Qing was sentenced to death, although her sentence was commuted to life in prison. Her story ended in 1991 when she committed suicide. She hung herself in the hospital room where she was temporarily being treated for cancer. She left a sad suicide note in which she lamented the changes that were coming to China. One of the chief architects of the Cultural Revolution was apparently dismayed at what she viewed as a backtracking of the revolution. She spoke of how revisionists had ruined China and put an end to the revolutionary ideals she had helped champion. This might have been the end of her story, but it was also the end of a very tumultuous and frightening chapter of Chinese history.

Chapter 9: A Strange Mix of Repression and Reform

"One-sidedness means thinking in terms of absolutes, that is, a metaphysical approach to problems. In the appraisal of our work, it is one-sided to regard everything either as all positive or all negative. To regard everything as positive is to see only the good and not the bad, and to tolerate only praise and no criticism. To talk as though our work is good in every respect is at variance with the facts. It is not true that everything is good; there are still shortcomings and mistakes. But neither is it true that everything is bad, and that, too, is at variance with the facts."

-Mao Zedong[1]

In the aftermath of Mao Zedong's demise in 1976, there was a major shift in both China's overall political direction and those who were running the government. A figure little known outside China but already trusted in the upper ranks of the Communist Party emerged as Mao's successor. Hua Guofeng, who had once worked in public security and risen steadily through provincial posts in Hunan, had been handpicked by Mao for senior leadership. By the mid-1970s, he was serving as premier and first vice chairman of the Communist Party. He was hardly an outsider in Beijing politics, though he was still a surprise choice to many observers.

---

[1] Zedong, Mao. *Quotations from Chairman Mao Tse-Tung (The Little Red Book).* Pg. 123.

In late 1978, more pragmatic heads prevailed. Under the leadership of Deng Xiaoping, China began charting a new course that deliberately distanced itself from Mao's most disastrous policies. Hua Guofeng's "Two Whatevers" line ("We will resolutely uphold whatever policy decisions Chairman Mao made, and unswervingly follow whatever instructions Chairman Mao gave") was quietly shelved, and the catastrophic Great Leap Forward was openly condemned. With Deng's emphasis on economic modernization and openness, the nation pivoted toward reforms that would shape China's trajectory for decades.

Correcting the disastrous agricultural policies of the Mao era proved to be a monumental task. It meant dismantling the communes and giving farmers more autonomy, paving the way for traditional farming and market-style exchanges in rural China. Instead of being forced to adhere strictly to government quotas (say, stocking eggs in bulk), farmers could now sell surplus produce freely, much like at a farmer's market. This return to localized markets and private enterprise, which was denounced by hardliners as dangerously capitalist, revived rural economies and brought family farms back to life.

This led to a great increase in agricultural profits that could be directly measured from 1979 to 1985. Farming improved, as did the environment. The 1970s saw the whole world begin to take a closer look at how human beings were affecting the environment. During this decade, for example, US President Richard Nixon established the Environmental Protection Agency (EPA).

By the end of the decade, the Chinese were starting to be better stewards as well. In sharp contrast to the days of killing sparrows, they had a much better grasp of the importance of sound environmental measures. This led to the passing of China's own Environmental Protection Law, which was focused on monitoring and enforcing environmental measures, in 1979.

By the time the 1970s came to a close and the 1980s dawned, China was back on the world stage in a big way. China had reestablished links with most major nations, even though it was still giving the cold shoulder to its former benefactor, the Soviet Union. Previous restraints on Chinese enterprise were slipping away, and new and exciting developments sprang up all over China. The gains made in the agricultural sector, in particular, allowed the Chinese government to mitigate many of the problems that had arisen in the urban sector.

However, in 1981, it became clear that the pace of investment needed to slow to prevent economic overheating. This did not sit well with old political hands who had championed massive industrial investment. They feared their benefits would be curtailed. The slowdown was temporary, though. By 1984, reforms were once again moving forward. Free enterprise was creating a competitive landscape in government and business, and price controls were being lifted in favor of market-based models.

Soon, new economic zones were being established in places like the Lower Yangtze, Fukien, and Kwangtung, where foreign investment was pouring in. In this new economic environment, bank loans suddenly took precedence over direct state funding. By 1985, even more reform measures were enacted, which brought even more benefits into the fields of both consumerism and industrial capacity.

Xiamen, one of the first special economic zones of China.[22]

Even so, since there was a decided lack of coordination, no standardization of the banking rules, and a bent toward inflation, some price controls had to be reintroduced in order to prevent long-term problems from erupting. This marked the return of some state controls on the Chinese economy.

As much as the Chinese experimented with a more liberal economy, the Chinese Communist Party remained relatively unchanged in its modus operandi. Unlike the Soviet Union, which was adopting its groundbreaking policy of glasnost (openness) and perestroika (restructuring) under Mikhail Gorbachev, the Chinese stuck to an authoritarian system that had little room for dissent or complaint.

The state of public affairs was decided to be wholly up to party officials and not something that could be democratically altered by the masses. This stronghold on Chinese society would prevent Chinese communism from totally collapsing. Unlike in Eastern Europe, there would be no toppling of Mao Zedong's statues in China.

Some scholars have argued that this sudden rush of economic liberalism after the crisis of the Cultural Revolution created a very strange situation in China. Suddenly, people were much better off, yet the communist leadership that had led them into the darkest of days was still in place.

Another interesting thing about China during this new period of openness was that many average Chinese citizens, for the first time ever, were getting a picture of how life in China compared to the rest of the world. Under Mao Zedong, the Chinese were faced with constant propaganda about how the capitalist countries of the world were evil and how the rest of the world's citizens were living in a state of slavery to greedy capitalists. The Chinese were now beginning to understand that much of the rest of the world was actually doing quite well and that their citizens were quite happy.

The Chinese began to look at their own country as it slowly rose from the economic and political wreckage of the past and realized just how far it lagged behind the developed world. This created a powerful desire to catch up, and there was a growing frustration with the slow pace of change among many young people. That frustration deepened in the spring of 1989 after the sudden death of reform-minded leader Hu Yaobang. His passing became the spark for massive demonstrations, which were led mostly by college students calling for political reform, greater freedoms, and an end to corruption. As weeks of peaceful protests unfolded in Beijing's Tiananmen Square, the world began to wonder if China might be on the brink of its own democratic breakthrough. But when the government sent in the army in early June, the result was a violent crackdown, forever cementing the events of 1989 as one of modern China's most infamous turning points.

The events of Tiananmen Square laid bare the chasm between China's intellectual elite and its ruling government. It seemed that this gap could not be bridged. Instead of dialogue, the state deployed troops, and the demonstrators were beaten—sometimes literally—into submission. In the aftermath, China's hardliners moved swiftly to roll back liberalization on every front.

This triggered a wave of international condemnation. The United States, Japan, and several European nations imposed sanctions, citing blatant human rights abuses. Yet, even within China's leadership, there was dissent. In 1992, Deng Xiaoping publicly broke with the hardliners, warning that their clampdowns had gone too far, particularly in reversing economic reforms that had begun to lift the country out of stagnation.

Deng's push to rein in the hardliners and revive economic reforms opened the door to a new chapter. The rest of the 1990s saw a steady return to relaxed controls, greater space for private enterprise, and, as a result, renewed prosperity. Southern China, in particular, experienced an economic boom, as private businesses flourished and fortunes were made almost overnight.

In his push to liberalize the economy of China, Deng often pointed to the example of Hong Kong. Hong Kong had been occupied by the British since the 19th century. The British would stick around until 1997, and even then, the economic and political system of their former colony was strikingly different than what was going on in China. Deng saw the economic prosperity in Hong Kong, and he used it as a model of how the rest of China should operate.

One of Deng's early supporters, Jiang Zemin, began to rise to prominence in the Chinese Communist Party. Jiang actually replaced high-profile Zhao Ziyang as general secretary in the immediate aftermath of the Tiananmen Square incident. He was also given the post of chairman of the Central Military Commission. Then, in 1993, he secured his place as president of the National People's Congress.

Deng had helped pave the way for Jiang to rise to power, and after Deng died in 1997, Jiang was able to further secure his grip, becoming China's paramount leader. Jiang presided over China during its momentous entry into the WTO (World Trade Organization) on December 11th, 2001. Interestingly, China became a member in the immediate aftermath of the World Trade Center attack in New York City, which took place on September 11th, 2001. Some historians have pointed out that it was during America's preoccupation with the 9/11 attacks and the subsequent war on terrorism that China truly rose to become a global power.

Chinese society was beginning to experience drastic changes due to one lingering holdover from Mao-style policies. Starting in 1979, China implemented its infamous one-child policy. This bit of social engineering was put in place to curb China's rapidly growing population and prevent a drain on resources. However, this policy led many Chinese families to try their hardest to have a son rather than a daughter. This was due to Chinese traditional thinking (which was never really eliminated by the Cultural Revolution) that a son was more preferable than a daughter. It was believed that boys took on a greater role as successors and, most importantly, as it pertained to their parents, in caring for the elderly.

Sadly, this led to many instances of aborted female babies so that families could produce that much-desired son. As the children of the one-child generation came of age in the 1990s, there was a noticeable imbalance between males and females. This, of course, would prove problematic when all of those sons found a very limited number of women available to marry.

Interestingly, another effect of the one-child policy was that for those who did choose to have a daughter and pinned all of the family hopes on that one child, there was a surge in empowerment and encouragement for these ambitious young women. The Communists always claimed to be champions of equality between males and females, and this new generation of females would put this proposed ideology to the test. Determined to do well and represent the interests of their families, Chinese universities were flooded with these young ladies who sought a good education and solid careers. As it turns out, even though most places in China might have had more boys than girls, Chinese colleges were perhaps the one place where girls were overrepresented.

Another effect of all of this was that a large number of girls who were not aborted ended up being given up for adoption. This was usually done by those who were still holding out for a male child. Parents did not register that they had a child with the state and then quietly dropped the baby off at the orphanage. As a result, orphanages swelled with all of these unwanted female babies.

Since the local Chinese were not likely to adopt them (that would defeat the whole purpose of seeking a male child), tremendous efforts were made to have these children adopted by parents from other countries, leading to large numbers of Chinese girls finding homes overseas. Demonstrating the reach of Maoist measures, the future of China had been significantly altered by this one policy alone.

Chapter 10: China During the 21st Century

"To be an official, you need to have the moral standing of an official—and that means not always thinking of yourself. A good cadre can be recognized by people no matter what their level is. Your constant thought needs to be, what can I do for the party? What will my legacy be?"

-Xi Jinping[i]

Deng's successor, Jiang Zemin, served as China's paramount leader from 1993 to 2003. He oversaw the British handover of Hong Kong in 1997, as well as the return of Macau from Portugal in 1999. He was the first Chinese leader to see the 21st century. He handed the reins of power over to his successor, Hu Jintao, who served from 2003 to 2013.

During Hu Jintao's regime, China gained more acceptance as an up-and-coming world power. Perception is everything, but hard, cold facts are pretty important too. No matter what anyone wanted to believe, China was making leaps and bounds as it pertained to its world standing. Financial statistics bear testament to this.

In 2007, China accounted for about 6 percent of the global gross domestic product—roughly one-sixteenth of the world's economy at the time. Since then, China's share has tripled to approximately 18 percent, firmly placing it second only to the United States.

---

[i] Brown, Kerry. *XI: A Study in Power*. 2022. Pg. 114.

One of China's crowning achievements during this period was hosting the 2008 Summer Olympics. Hu's time in office was known for its positive international trends, and it has been dubbed the *hexie* or "harmony" period by the Chinese. This was also due to the fact that Hu constantly referred to the need for a Socialist Harmonious Society. This was his answer to widening inequality and social unrest.

However, not everything was as harmonious as Hu and the government would have liked it to be. The very year China was stepping onto the world stage to host the 2008 Olympics, dramatic riots and protests took place in Tibet. Tibetans were wary of Chinese rule and sought to take advantage of international scrutiny over the Olympics to gain worldwide attention to their cause. There was widespread destruction of property during the unrest. Many people were injured, and some were even killed. The Chinese government pushed back hard against the rioters, and people were arrested in large numbers. The Chinese Communist Party also put a curfew in place to ensure that further unrest was quelled.

The crackdown in Tibet led to a larger police presence in Tibet's urban population centers. Much like an occupying army, armored units patrolled nonstop, making sure no one got out of line. They were not only on the lookout for protesters carrying signs or even rioters destroying property. They were also looking for Tibetan monks setting themselves on fire. As a form of ultimate protest, Tibetan monks were willing to set themselves ablaze in an act of self-immolation. The Chinese, ever conscious of their image, most certainly did not want the world to see such things play out on their television screens. China wished to present itself as a rising political and economic power. They had no room for Tibetan dissidents in their ambitious plans for the future.

The internet factored largely into China's renewed push for modernization. But almost immediately, the Chinese communist government faced the difficulty of trying to rein in or even censor what the average Chinese citizen was seeing on the internet. From unwanted news reports to pornographic material, Chinese officials were determined to monitor and, if necessary, censor what the Chinese had access to on the web.

This effort to safeguard the Chinese from objectionable (at least objectionable to the Chinese Communist Party) content would become known as the Great Firewall of China. Hot button topics such as the Dalai Lama and the Tiananmen Square incident, for example, were blocked and kept firmly on the outside of this Great Firewall. The Great Firewall consisted of real-time human monitors who constantly examined materials being disseminated and software deployed on Chinese home computers that was designed to block questionable material. As of this writing, this system of censorship and surveillance is still in place.

Interestingly, in 2015, China's efforts to monitor its citizens online took a new turn. Alongside traditional internet censorship, new programs emerged that tracked and assessed certain aspects of people's behavior, particularly their financial reliability and legal compliance. While other countries have long relied on credit scores to measure one's ability to borrow money, China began piloting what became known as the Social Credit System. In practice, this was not a single, all-encompassing score but a patchwork of local government blacklists and private platforms, such as Alibaba's voluntary "Sesame Credit," that rewarded trustworthy conduct. The higher one's standing, the more conveniences and opportunities became available, from easier access to loans to waived deposits. Of course, the reverse could also be true for those who fell afoul of the rules, especially if they ignored court orders or failed to pay debts. The internet being what it is, one might imagine the system punishing people for disapproved hobbies, but these claims, such as fans of Japanese anime or video games being penalized, remain unsubstantiated.

This modern Social Credit System is not entirely new. It echoes an ancient Chinese tradition. During the medieval era, Daoist priests and later literati used ledgers of merit and demerit (*gongguoge*). These were papers or booklets in which people recorded daily good and bad deeds that were tabulated as moral points. Over the centuries, especially from the Song through the Qing dynasties, these ledgers became more widespread, not just as spiritual diaries but as frameworks for moral self-improvement and social guidance. Only now, with the technological infrastructure backed by state power, are comparable metrics being applied at scale but with vastly greater reach, impact, and enforcement.

In 2012, Hu Jintao's administration gave way to Chinese President Xi Jinping. Working from the same playbook as his predecessors, Xi Jinping came to prominence by becoming the head of his party, the head of the state, and the head of the army. This meant that he had political and governmental control, as well as solid military backing.

President Xi Jinping.³⁸

President Xi's first few years were busy ones, as he embarked upon a wide range of initiatives. By 2018, Xi Jinping must have thought he still had plenty more left to do. That year, under his leadership, China's National People's Congress amended the constitution to remove the two-term limit for the presidency, opening the door for him to rule for as long as he chooses. Since then, Xi has wielded his authority with full force, consolidating power across the party, state, and military. He shows no signs of reversing course.

Under the ambitious rule of Xi Jinping, China embarked upon one of its greatest initiatives since Mao Zedong's Great Leap Forward. Dubbed the Belt and Road Initiative, this program sought to link China with other markets by creating infrastructure in foreign countries, such as roads and railways, to better distribute Chinese goods to places such as Africa, India, central Asia, and the Middle East.

The Great Leap Forward had focused on building up the infrastructure of China, but the Belt and Road Initiative turned outward. However, this was not just out of China's own kind-hearted beneficence. These road-building projects were created to bring China lucrative new markets in the places where the roads were being built. It also allowed for better transport of certain raw materials that China might want to ship along those roads and rail lines.

China, for example, has been widely criticized for its resource deals in Africa, especially in its pursuit of critical minerals such as cobalt and copper. These materials are essential for modern electronics and green technologies. These ventures often spark accusations of exploitation, with profits and benefits flowing disproportionately back to China. Yet, despite these motives, Beijing has also been praised for financing and building key infrastructure, from highways and railways to ports and power plants, bringing development to regions long overlooked by other global powers.

Even though the rest of the world might remain skeptical of the Chinese Communist Party's motives, Chinese officials wished to present China as a benign force for good on the world stage. Much like the United States was known for its efforts to aid struggling nation-states, China also wanted to create the appearance of a strong nation reaching down to help those who were less fortunate.

However, by the early 2020s, two big controversies would badly tarnish China's image. The first of these controversies centered on growing speculation over the fate of China's Uyghur Muslims. The Uyghurs are a Turkic people who have lived for centuries in China's far western Xinjiang region. While concerns about their treatment reached global headlines in the 2020s, reports describing the construction of sprawling "re-education" facilities stretch back to the 2010s. These centers, according to human rights groups, were aimed at erasing Uyghur customs and religious practices and replacing them with loyalty to the Chinese Communist Party.

In 2019, Chinese officials claimed many "trainees" had "graduated" and that some facilities had closed, but independent evidence suggested the network remained largely intact. To counter criticism, Beijing organized tightly controlled tours for diplomats and journalists, insisting its programs in Xinjiang were purely vocational and designed to combat extremism. Even so, new accusations in the 2020s again alleged widespread detention, mistreatment, and forced labor. China continues to reject these claims.

It was also in the early 2020s that the world was rocked by a global pandemic. While many aspects of the pandemic remain fiercely debated, the first major outbreak was detected in Wuhan, China, before spreading rapidly across the globe. The precise origin of the virus, whether from a natural spillover or another source, remains unproven. Still, critics have accused Chinese authorities of responding too slowly in the earliest days, allowing the outbreak to worsen. Considering how devastating the pandemic was to nations such as Iran, Russia, Britain, and the United States, some are surprised that the diplomatic blowback against Beijing has not been greater.

In theory, these nations could have united to condemn China or even demand some form of reparations. In practice, world leaders have largely settled for muted statements, while Chinese officials maintain they acted decisively. The WHO (World Health Organization) has echoed some of these assurances, though its own conduct during the pandemic drew heavy scrutiny and eroded public trust.

Even years later, the actions of both China and the WHO remain the subject of ongoing debate but not outright condemnation. While talk of holding China accountable surfaces from time to time, it remains firmly in the realm of speculation rather than action.

The general acceptance—grudging though it may be—of China's muted response to the global pandemic is perhaps one of the clearest signs of how far China's global standing has come. In the 19th and early 20th centuries, even a minor dispute involving China could provoke demands for immediate compensation. Under the Boxer Protocol, foreign powers wielded overwhelming leverage over Beijing.

Yet today, China could be the location of the first-known outbreak of a pandemic that crippled economies and disrupted lives across the planet, and it still faces no coordinated sanctions or demands for reparations. This change in attitude may have much to do with the powerful cards China holds—its political influence, its deep integration into global supply chains, and the economic dependencies it has cultivated with governments worldwide.

Iran offers a telling example. As a predominantly Muslim nation, one might expect it to voice concern over allegations of mass detention and repression of Uyghur Muslims in Xinjiang. Not long ago, Iran's supreme leader issued a fatwa (a legal ruling on Islamic law) against novelist Salman Rushdie for perceived insults to Islam. However, in the case of alleged abuses against Uyghurs, Tehran has remained silent. Deepening economic links with Beijing, along with possible strategic and military considerations, may explain this.

In fact, Iran was among the nations that sent parliamentary delegations to Xinjiang. The Iranian officials emerged from these tightly managed tours with public praise for China's "counter-terrorism" and "vocational training" programs. That endorsement is striking in light of history. Over a thousand years ago, during the Islamic conquest of Persia, parts of what is now Xinjiang saw waves of migrants and traders from Persian lands. This historical connection makes Tehran's unwillingness to support the Uyghurs today all the more remarkable.

Whether the Iranian delegations genuinely saw nothing amiss or simply chose not to acknowledge it, the outcome is the same. There were no follow-up investigations, no calls for accountability, and no break from Beijing's official narrative. Whatever is happening in Xinjiang remains behind a carefully maintained curtain, and Iran seems content to play its part in keeping it closed.

As you can see, China's ability to shape narratives now extends far beyond its borders. Corporations, athletes, and celebrities have all publicly backtracked after crossing Beijing's political red lines. China has long censored its own people, but the fact that its pressure can reach into the supposedly free press of other nations is remarkable.

Nevertheless, right or wrong, China and the Chinese Communist Party still stand strong. The Chinese Communist Party actually celebrated its 100th anniversary on July 1st, 2021. During an official event that was ostensibly meant to be a celebration, President Xi Jinping had some rather harsh and stark words for the rest of the world. He gave a speech in which he bluntly stated that any outside power attempting to interfere with China and Chinese policies would have their "heads bashed in."[i] His comment was apparently meant to be a vivid metaphor—an expression of China's growing resolve to defend its sovereignty and national interests in the face of foreign interference. Even so, it was clear to everyone listening that this was not the China of old and that it would not be pushed around.

China has a long history of being bullied and pushed around by outside powers. Whether it was the Mongols, the British, or the Japanese, foreign interference has left deep scars. In that light, it is understandable that Xi Jinping might frame his warnings to the outside world in sober, uncompromising terms. In earlier centuries, when China resisted invasions or foreign domination, its defiance was rooted in genuine self-defense. However, future instances of what Beijing deems "interference" may not be so morally clear-cut.

---

[i] Brown, Kerry. *XI: A Study in Power.* Pg. 293.

Xi's language, for example, could just as easily be aimed at nations merely voicing concern over China's treatment of Uyghurs in Xinjiang. Beijing may dispute these allegations, but the notion that no one can even question Chinese actions pushes beyond defensive nationalism into an effort to shut down legitimate international scrutiny. Then there is the specter of Taiwan. If Chinese policy were to escalate to the bombing of Taiwan followed by a bloody invasion, Xi's warning would imply that outsiders should stand aside and let it happen, or risk, in his words, getting their "heads bashed" against a "Great Wall of steel."

It must be remembered that during his speech marking the Chinese Communist Party's 100th anniversary in July 2021, Xi was playing to a domestic audience full of senior party officials. Projecting toughness before such an audience was politically useful. Yet the entire world was also watching, and the force of his words rippled far beyond Tiananmen Square. That undercurrent still lingers as the international community watches with growing unease, waiting to see how this latest chapter in Chinese history will unfold.

Conclusion:
China—An Exercise in Strategic Patience

China is one of the oldest, continuous civilizations on the planet. Needless to say, it has gone through quite a few twists and turns in its history. China rose to prominence early on as the Middle Kingdom, with many satellite kingdoms surrounding it. Yet, even mighty China was ultimately overcome by the Mongol horde and made into just another piece of the Mongol khanate under the Yuan dynasty.

Although China was occupied by the Mongols, the undercurrent of Chinese civilization still survived. The Mongols remained impressed by China's Song dynasty—so much so that they sought to emulate it in their Yuan dynasty. The Mongols made use of Chinese inventions such as paper, rockets, gunpowder, and currency to shore up the strength of their own empire.

The Chinese spirit of innovation that brought about these great inventions was not going to abide Mongol occupation and usurpation forever. Eventually, the Chinese threw off their Mongolian yoke, which gave way to the majestic Ming dynasty. The Ming was arguably one of the greatest of all the Chinese dynasties.

Over time, the Ming dynasty weakened, and the Qing, whose leaders originated in Manchuria, overcame it. Some Ming loyalists went to Taiwan, where they tried to create their own alternative version of China. This state did not last, and soon the Qing controlled all of China and Taiwan.

It is striking to consider how often Taiwan has stood at a crossroads in China's destiny. The Ming loyalists once retreated here, holding out for two decades before the Qing took the island. Centuries later, the Qing themselves lost Taiwan to Japan. Then, in 1949, after years of brutal civil war, Chiang Kai-shek's Nationalists repeated history, retreating to Taiwan as the Communists consolidated power on the mainland.

Yet there is one major difference. Where the Ming lasted only a short while, the current government in Taiwan has endured for over seventy years, becoming an alternative Chinese state with its own identity and institutions. The Chinese Communist Party still insists Taiwan is an inalienable part of China, destined for "reunification," by force if necessary. That claim has kept the Taiwan question alive as one of the most enduring and dangerous issues in modern geopolitics.

If Beijing truly intends to seize Taiwan, and if Taiwan's allies, most notably the United States, are equally serious about its defense, the world could find itself staring at the fault line of a major war. Recent events show just how quickly such fault lines can rupture. Russia's invasion of Ukraine in 2022 and the renewed fighting between Israel and Hamas have both shaken the global order. A Taiwan conflict could be just as destabilizing—perhaps more so.

A war across the Taiwan Strait could draw in the US Navy, Japanese forces, and potentially South Korea. That, in turn, could tempt North Korea to side with Beijing and strike at its old enemies in the south. In 2024, North Korea and Russia signed a mutual aid treaty that was vague enough to leave Moscow wiggle room but concrete enough to raise the specter of Russian involvement in any East Asian war. If that happened, the world could face China, North Korea, and Russia as aligned combatants. With all three possessing nuclear weapons, with Russia having the largest arsenal in the world, the dangers would rise to existential levels.

And yet, perhaps it is precisely this idea of catastrophe that has so far stayed Beijing's hand. Chinese leaders know the risks as well as anyone. For now, they are practicing strategic patience, keeping the Taiwan question unresolved rather than igniting a war that could spiral beyond control. For the sake of China, Taiwan, and the rest of the world, one can only hope that patience endures.

Part 2: Chinese Folktales and Legends

An Enthralling Collection of Stories, Heroes, Magical Creatures, and Timeless Tales from Ancient China

How to Pronounce Pinyin

"Pinyin" means "spelled sounds." Chinese children spend years learning Chinese characters, but pinyin spells out the sounds in Chinese words phonetically. Learning the basics of pinyin will enable you to read the Chinese words in this book. (We will not worry about tone marks.)

Consonants

The consonants b, d, f, g, h, j, k, l, m, n, p, and t are pronounced like they are in English. Here is a basic guide to the other consonant sounds:

"j" sounds like the "j" in "jet"

"q" has a "ch" sound, so the word "Qin" sounds like "cheen"

"x" has an "sh" sound, so "Xian" sounds like "Shee ahn"

"zh" has a "j" sound with a flat tongue

"ch" is like the English "ch" but with a flat tongue

"sh" is like the English "sh" but with a flat tongue

"r" is like the English "r" but the tongue curls slightly back

"z" sounds like the "ds" in "birds"

"c" sounds like the "ts" sound in "bats"

"s" sounds like the "s" in "sun"

Vowels

"a" is like the "ah" sound in "father"

"o" sounds like the "oh" sound in "go"

"e" sounds like the short "e" in "pen"

"i" sounds like the long "e" in "see" (the word "Pinyin" sounds like peen yeen)

"u" sounds like the "oo" sound in "food"

Introduction

"Yeye! Yeye! Tell us a story! Please?"

The grandfather sat on his stool and lit his cigarette as the cousins pulled their stools close to him in the courtyard. The older children held the toddlers on their laps as evening approached. Behind them, the adults cleared the tables and squatted to wash dishes in basins on the courtyard floor. It was Chūnjié, the Chinese New Year, also known as Spring Festival. The extended family had gathered to celebrate in the ancestral village, as they had done for centuries. The grown-ups smiled as they glanced at the grandfather, surrounded by the children. Sharing their folklore was an essential element of their festivals.

"And what story shall I tell you, dear children?"

"Sun Wukong! Monkey King! Monkey King!" the children squealed.

"Monkey King? It's always Monkey King! I told you a Monkey King story yesterday and the day before! Tonight, I shall tell a different story that took place long before the Monkey King. It is the story of Pangu, who formed the universe, and Nuwa, who created people and repaired the sky."

"Was the sky broken?" asked a child.

"Yes, it was. And tonight, you'll learn what happened."

Just as Chinese grandparents have shared their legends for millennia, this book immerses readers in the rich tapestry of ancient China's myths and folklore. It vividly brings the enchanting tales of heroes and magical creatures to life. These ancient stories highlight the cultural, spiritual, and historical depth of Chinese traditions. They are not simply fairy tales; in fact, most dive into China's ancient history, where real people and events gained mythical status. The challenge is separating myth from reality.

These folktales introduce readers to Chinese insights and proverbs. China's people believe their history and mythology hold valuable life lessons and universal wisdom. Even today, their speech is full of idioms and catchphrases from these tales. Readers will enjoy the linguistic cleverness of these ancient stories through puns and other wordplay. Typical Chinese self-deprecating humor, subtle irony, witty dialogue, and layered meanings shine through these legends that readers of all ages can enjoy.

This book organizes Chinese folklore thematically into ten chapters, introducing key Chinese concepts such as yin and yang, the five elements, the phoenix, and the symbolism of the lotus. It brings characters like the Jade Emperor, the Monkey King, and the Dragon King to life. Readers will meet quasi-historical characters, such as Yu the Engineer, who introduced effective flood control measures and became the first emperor of the Xia dynasty. Magic, adventure, dashed hopes, realized dreams, and so much more await the reader in the coming chapters.

Chapter 1:
China's Folkloric Foundations

This chapter delves into the foundational myths and legends that lay the groundwork for China's rich folklore tradition. These stories offer invaluable insight into how the ancient Chinese perceived cosmic order and the world's origins. For instance, how did they think the universe and humanity came into being? Who established the world's natural and moral order? As we discuss these myths, remember that the Chinese had multiple versions of the stories.

How did the universe begin? According to Chinese mythology, before time began, nothing existed but a dark, chaotic void. The swirling chaos formed an egg, which contained the entire universe within a tiny space. It also held yin and yang: the opposite yet interconnected forces of balance and duality. Yang represents day, brightness, movement, and height (as in a mountain), while yin represents night, darkness, rest, and a closed door. Within the egg, yin and yang struggled against each other. Ultimately, they achieved balance for the first time, forming a hairy, horned, rotund dwarf named Pangu.

Pangu carried a giant axe, which he cracked the egg. As Pangu broke out of the egg, the universe also broke free. Pangu swung his axe, separating yin and yang, creating the Earth and sky. He stood on the Earth and held up the sky, which gradually rose higher as the Earth grew thicker. The longer Pangu held up the sky, the taller he grew, until he became a mighty giant.

The presence of Shangdi, China's supreme deity, is implied in the formation of the primeval egg. His name means "primordial, first, and highest." He was the ultimate great power, ruling over a hierarchy of other gods who emerged later in Chinese mythology. Shangdi transcended the material universe and physical laws.

At the Border Sacrifice, the emperor sacrificed a sheep or bull to Shangdi while reciting the following:

> "Of old, in the beginning, there was the great chaos, without form and dark. The five elements [planets] had not begun to revolve, nor the sun and moon to shine. You, O Spiritual Sovereign, first divided the grosser parts from the purer. You made Heaven. You made Earth. You made man. All things with their reproducing power got their being."[i]

The ancient Chinese believed that when their kings died, their souls merged with the supreme deity, Shangdi. Thus, the Chinese worshipped their ancestral kings, asking them to mediate with Shangdi. They believed Heaven (Tian) and Shangdi were essentially the same. Heaven was not so much a place as an abstract, cosmic force. The Chinese philosopher Mozi (408-382 BCE), who founded the Mohist school of thought, said this about Tian (or Shangdi):

> "I know Heaven (Tian) loves men dearly, not without reason. Heaven ordered the sun, the moon, and the stars to enlighten and guide them. Heaven ordained the four seasons, Spring, Autumn, Winter, and Summer, to regulate them. Heaven sent down snow, frost, rain, and dew to grow the five grains, flax, and silk so that the people could use and enjoy them. Heaven established the hills, rivers, ravines, and valleys, and arranged many things to minister to man's good or bring him evil."[ii]

Once Pangu hatched, divine creatures known as the "Four Benevolent Animals" arrived to assist him. They were the Dragon, Phoenix, Qilin, and Turtle. We will discuss the Dragon and the Phoenix in chapters five and seven. Together, these four creatures represented the Chinese constellations.

---

[i] James Legge, *The Notions of the Chinese Concerning Gods and Spirits* (Hong Kong Register, 1852), 28.

[ii] *The Works of Motze*, (Confucius Publishing Co., 1980), 290.

Artwork of the Turtle, or Black Tortoise, often shows a snake coiled around it. It was the "Black Warrior of the North." The Qilin had the body of a fiery horse (or goat) with cloven hooves and the head and tail of a dragon. It symbolized prosperity and good luck. When the Qilin appeared, it was an omen of the birth or death of a sage or an exceptional ruler.

The Qilin [14]

Eventually, Pangu died, and his body became the four pillars that supported the sky. By this time, other gods and goddesses had emerged. The Chinese believed certain mortals became gods after death, and Pangu was among those. They thought their deities lived in palaces on sacred mountains. One ancient deity was Gonggong, the water god. He had red hair, a human face, and a snake's body. Zhurong was the god of fire, yet he was known for doing nothing and desiring nothing. However, one day, he did do something.

Gonggong wanted to usurp the throne of Heaven and rule the cosmos. Zhurong sprang into action to stop him. The two gods clashed in a ferocious, protracted war, fighting in both Heaven and Earth. Zhurong finally won the battle, preserving Heaven's order. Gonggong was furious. He smashed his head against Mount Buzhou, one of the four pillars that held up the sky. When the sky collapsed, it opened Heaven's flood gates, and the Great Flood ensued.

Ancient China had two variations of when the Great Flood happened. Some accounts say it was a universal flood that occurred shortly after the world's creation. Other stories say it was a localized but horrific and prolonged flooding of the river system between the Yellow River and the Yangtze at the beginning of the Xia dynasty. In both cases, Gonggong was to blame. Chapter five will cover the second version, in which Yu the Engineer saved the day. This chapter unwraps the first version.

After Pangu died, his body not only formed the four pillars that hold up the sky (the four great mountains), but also gave rise to the rivers, plants, and animals. Huaxu was a goddess who emerged from Pangu's body. After stepping into a footprint of Lei Shen, the thunder god, Huaxu became pregnant and gave birth to Fuxi and his sister, Nuwa. Like their mother, the twins had human heads and serpent bodies. When Gonggong caused the Great Flood, Nuwa collected five colored stones from the river, melted them, and repaired the broken sky.

However, Fuxi and Nuwa were the only creatures that survived the flood. Fuxi turned to Nuwa. "We need to marry and repopulate the earth," he said.

"We can't marry!" Nuwa replied. "You're my brother!"

"Okay. We'll let Heaven decide. You climb that mountain, and I'll climb this one. Each of us will light a fire. If the smoke rises straight up, that means we should not get married. But if the smoke from my fire travels toward your mountain and the smoke from your fire comes out to meet it, that means that Heaven approves our marriage."

The smoke from the two fires merged, so the twins married and repopulated the earth. However, they did not do it in the usual way. With Fuxi's assistance, Nuwa created animals. On day one, she made chickens. The next day, she created dogs. On the third day, she made sheep, and on the fourth, pigs. She made cows on the fifth day and horses on the sixth.

A Tang dynasty painting of Nuwa and Fuxi[25]

Finally, on the seventh day, Nuwa took yellow clay and formed two creatures with faces that resembled hers and Fuxi's: a man and a woman. She gave all her creations the ability to reproduce.

After people had lived on the earth for many years, they formed tribes that often fought each other for power. Huangdi (Yellow Emperor), China's legendary first emperor, was one of the "Five Great Emperors" of China. Chinese history claims he ruled a group of tribes from 2679 to 2597 BCE in north-central China. Written history that has survived to modern times does not mention him until the early fourth century BCE. However, the Chinese did not begin writing until about 1,400 years after the Yellow Emperor's reign. Although he probably was a real person, all the exploits attributed to him place Huangdi in legendary status. By the Han dynasty (which began in 202 BCE), followers of the Taoist religion worshipped him as a god.

The Yellow Emperor's given name was Xuan Yuan. Legend says that when he was conceived, a loud thunderclap rang out even though it was a clear day. As a young man, Huangdi was a farmer who learned to tame animals, like the bear and tiger. He taught his followers to build houses, grow grains, domesticate animals, make clothing, and sail in boats. (The ancient Mesopotamians had been doing all those things for at least two millennia.) Huangdi supposedly invented wheeled carts, but, once again, the Sumerians of southern Mesopotamia (Iraq) were already using chariots in his lifetime. He might have introduced these things to China, but Huangdi was not their first inventor.

Huangdi's path to becoming an emperor over multiple tribes began when he was the leader of the Youxiong (Bear) tribe, which warred against the Shennong (Bull) tribe. After the Youxiong tribe won, the two tribes united under the leadership of Huangdi, marking the beginning of Chinese civilization. However, a superhuman tribe, led by Chi You, challenged Huangdi's people. Chi You and his eighty-one brothers each had four eyes and eight arms. Huangdi formed a coalition with eight nearby tribes, yet the ensuing battle dragged on for days, with neither side taking the lead.

Huangdi's forces finally got the upper hand, but Chi You puffed a thick fog from his nostrils that blocked the sun. No one could see anything. In a panic, Huangdi's army tried to leave the battlefield but wandered around aimlessly in the mist. Just in time, Huangdi invented the "south-pointing" chariot, building it right there on the field despite the fog obscuring everything. The chariot's mechanisms pointed south, so he led his men away from the battle. Yet, before Huangdi and his me made their escape, Chi You used his black magic to call up a fierce storm. Huangdi prayed to the gods, and they dispersed the storm, enabling Huangdi to triumph over Chi You and his diabolical tribe.

What was the south-pointing chariot? It was a real thing, but Huangdi did not invent it. Horses and chariots did not appear in China until the Shang dynasty (1600–1046 BCE). An engineer named Ma Jun is credited with inventing the south-pointing chariot in the third century BCE. It was a two-wheeled chariot with gear and track ratios and a specific wheel size, which always kept a figure attached to the wheels pointing south. The south-pointing chariot was well-documented in Chinese histories, with detailed descriptions of its mechanics.

According to later tales, the Yellow Emperor was a sage who accomplished an incredible number of inventions. He reportedly developed traditional Chinese medicine, and it worked so well for him that he lived to be a hundred years old. He supposedly wrote China's first medical book; however, writing did not emerge in China until the Shang dynasty (1600–1046 BCE). Other innovations that legend says Huangdi introduced include the Chinese calendar, advanced mathematics, Chinese astronomy, coins, and China's first law code.

The Huangdi Temple in Xinzheng City, Henan Province [36]

Tradition also says the Yellow Emperor invented Cuju, a Chinese ball game that blended elements from today's soccer and basketball. Cuju was the world's first kicking game. The teams had to keep the ball in the air without touching it with their hands and kick it through a hoop in the center of the court. Intriguingly, the ancient Olmecs and other Mesoamerican tribes had an almost identical game, which the Aztecs called Ulama.

Taoism, a philosophical and religious system that developed in the sixth century BCE, elevated Huangdi to a deity. Taoists credited him with establishing the natural and moral order of the world by bringing harmony between Earth and Heaven. He achieved this by uniting the tribes to defeat the Chi You tribe, bringing peace and eliminating evil. Huangdi exemplified the core Chinese principles of harmony, cohesion, and respect for authority. The Chinese considered him the ideal ruler, who led with virtue, wisdom, moral integrity, and a keen understanding of natural law.

Taoists said he balanced "Wuxing," the Five Elements (wood, fire, earth, metal, water) that explain the universe's relationships and interactions. Each element is associated with specific parts of the body, influencing Chinese traditional medicine.

The first element, wood, represents new beginnings, growth, and flexibility. Springtime and the color green are associated with this element. The body parts connected to the element of wood are the gallbladder and liver. The second element, fire, represents energy and passion. Summer and the color red are linked to this element. Its body parts are the heart and the small intestine.

Earth is the third element, symbolizing nurture, stability, and practicality. It is connected to late summer and the color yellow. The pancreas, spleen, and stomach are the body parts associated with Earth. The fourth element is metal, representing structure, strength, and order. It is associated with autumn and the color white. Its body parts are the large intestine and lungs. The fifth element is water, representing emotion, flexibility, and wisdom. Water is connected to winter and the color black, and its body parts are the bladder and kidneys.

One of the Yellow Emperor's wives, Leizu, was also exceptionally innovative. One day, she was sitting in her garden, drinking tea in the shade of a mulberry tree. A sudden breeze caused the cocoon of a silkworm moth to fall out of the tree. Plop! It landed in Leizu's hot tea.

Leizu looked at the cocoon and noticed it was dissolving. Curious, she stuck her finger in the tea and pulled on the unraveling string. It was over three hundred feet long.

Empress Leizu told her husband about the silk thread from the cocoon. "It is lustrous and smooth! I wonder if I can weave it into cloth?"

Huangdi nodded and smiled. "By all means, investigate this matter!"

Leizu explored the mulberry trees in her garden, studying the silkworms' life cycle, learning how to raise them. She discovered that female silkworm moths laid hundreds of eggs on mulberry leaves, and when the larvae hatched, they immediately began feeding on the leaves. After growing and molting several times over three weeks, the silkworms raised their upper bodies off the leaves and started swaying. The empress learned this was the time to gather them onto frames, as each caterpillar would soon form a cocoon of silk thread.

Leizu's workers put the cocoons in boiling water and unraveled the silk. She also invented a reel for winding the thread, which would be dyed and woven into cloth on a silk loom, another of Leizu's inventions. The Chinese kept their silk-making process as a state secret, which gave them a monopoly on the silk textile trade for centuries.

Court ladies pound silk cloth to soften it. [27]

Chapter 2:
The Jade Emperor's Realm

Who was the Jade Emperor? He was the supreme deity in Taoist mythology. He headed a celestial hierarchy with a pantheon of gods and goddesses under him. The Jade Emperor was a pivotal figure who governed the heavens and the Earth. Was he the same as Shangdi? How did he rise to power and maintain order and justice among the gods? This chapter dives into these questions and also investigates other significant deities in his court.

China's Spring and Autumn period (772-476 BCE) was a tumultuous time in the Zhou dynasty when vassal kings took advantage of weak emperors. Despite messy politics, China's culture flourished under the "Hundred Schools of Thought," an era when several major philosophies emerged under the teachings of K'ung (Confucius), Laozi (Lao Tzu), and Mozi. Laozi developed Taoism (Daoism), possibly influenced by earlier teachings.

Taoism was a philosophy that later developed into a religion. Laozi taught that "Dao," or "the Way," governed the universe, bringing natural order. Dao (Tao) was not a deity but a fundamental principle, the underlying force that creates and sustains harmony and balance. Laozi never mentioned the Jade Emperor. He was more concerned with the philosophical side of things—most importantly, achieving oneness with Dao. He said that oneness with Dao occurred when a person remained uninvolved with the things of the world, lived a simple life, disregarded self-interest, and had no attachments to anything.

Laozi wrote the *Tao-Te-Ching* (*The Book of the Way*), a poetic guide about emptying oneself of pride and yielding to life's ups and downs. As time passed, Laozi's followers struggled with not worshiping anything. Yes, Dao was a divine principle, but one cannot offer sacrifices to a principle. To whom should they pray? Over the centuries, Taoism evolved into a religion with gods and goddesses. Emperor Xuanzong (712-756 CE) declared it the state religion of the Tang dynasty and mandated that everyone study Taoist scriptures. He elevated Laozi to the status of a royal ancestor and established a school for Taoist teachers.

This was when the Jade Emperor became the most important god in Taoism. Before the Tang dynasty, he was unknown or perhaps a deity in Chinese folk religion. Now, he

Ming dynasty silk painting of the Jade Emperor [28]

was Heaven's king. The Chinese referred to their supreme deity as "Yu Huang Shangdi" or "Jade Emperor, the highest god." In the Tang dynasty, the Jade Emperor was a manifestation of Shangdi. He ruled the cosmos and lived in the highest Heaven with his family and officials in a splendid palace.

One tradition regarding the Jade Emperor's origins said he was always a god. Another said he was a man who became a god. In the second version, he was a soldier and minor official named Zhang Denglai. He died in the 1046 BCE Battle of Muye that ended the Shang dynasty and began the Zhou dynasty. He and the other soldiers who died were at the "Terrace of Canonization" in the afterlife. A deceased nobleman named Jiang Ziya was passing out rewards—positions in Heaven's hierarchy—for those who were the most valiant in the battle. He filled all the positions but one, the Jade Emperor.

Jiang Ziya coveted the Jade Emperor's position, but it would be unseemly to appoint himself, so he waited for the other soldiers to offer it to him. When they did, he modestly replied, "Děng lái" ("Wait a second"). He did not want to appear too eager. However, in Chinese, "Denglai" was also the name of the brave soldier. (This is one example of puns in Chinese stories.) Zhang Denglai stepped forward to receive the reward, and Jiang Ziya could not lose face. He had no choice but to award Zhang Denglai the position of Jade Emperor.

Another Jade Emperor origin story took place in the Kingdom of Miraculous Joy and Heavenly Lights. The aged, infirm king had no sons, so his queen prayed for a son to be the crown prince. One night, she dreamed of the philosopher Laozi and miraculously conceived. (Inexplicable, conceptions were a common theme in Chinese folklore.) The baby was surprisingly advanced for his age. He walked and talked much earlier than ordinary babies.

The child impressed everyone with his calmness, gentleness, and concern for others. He helped the poor and disabled, and was respectful to everyone high and low, even the animals. When the king died, the prince became king. After stabilizing and enriching his kingdom, he journeyed to the Bright and Fragrant Cliff to meditate, study, and cultivate Dao. He achieved his aim and became immortal.

As an immortal, the king became an assistant to Yuanshi Tianzun, "Heaven's Lord of Primordial Beginnings" (probably Shangdi). One of his duties was to assist the people of Earth in fighting demons. The most powerful demon had recruited an army of malevolent spirits to conquer Heaven and rule the universe. The gods rallied to defend Heaven, but he overcame them.

The Jade Emperor saw an ominous glow in Heaven and flew upward to challenge the formidable demon. In a horrendous battle in which the mountains quaked and tidal waves swept the seas, the Jade Emperor defeated the daunting demon and scattered his hellish horde. In Chinese mythology, Heaven's rulers did not reign forever. Yuanshi Tianzun appointed the Jade Emperor to succeed him as the supreme god of Heaven, where he maintained order and justice among the gods.

Even today, Taoists and Buddhists worship the Jade Emperor on the ninth day of the Chinese New Year. They burn incense and offer vegetables, cakes, fruit, and wine on an altar decorated with paper lanterns. Worshippers kneel and prostrate themselves before his image in their homes or Taoist temples.

The Jade Emperor's wife was Wang Mu, and the couple had seven daughters. One of their daughters was Zhinu, the weaver goddess. Her job was to weave the colorful sunsets and the Silver River (Milky Way). Every day, with her magical robe, Zhinu flew down to Earth to bathe in a stream. A herdsman named Niu Lang saw her and was enchanted by her beauty. He snatched her magic robe, which she used to travel between Earth and Heaven.

"Bù kě néng! (No way!)" Zhinu screeched. "Give me back my robe! I can't get back to Heaven without it."

"What about Heaven on Earth?" the saucy shepherd asked. "Come to my house and be my bride!"

Zhinu cocked her head and looked at the handsome herdsman. She shrugged and went with him. When the Jade Emperor heard, he was livid. Yet, his daughter was with the shepherd of her own free will.

After some time, Zhinu found the chest where her husband had hidden the magic robe. She was lonely for her parents and her home in Heaven, so she used the robe to visit them. Once she arrived in Heaven, the Jade Emperor threw the Silver River (Milky Way) between Heaven and Earth. Zhinu had woven it, and now it blocked her way back to her shepherd.

However, the Jade Emperor was touched by his daughter's wails when she could not return to her husband. "Sweet daughter, you belong here, but once a year, you can visit your shepherd. I will make a bridge over the Silver River on the seventh day of the seventh moon each year."

The Lyra constellation is east of the Milky Way, and the star Vega represents Zhinu. The Aquila constella-

Chang'e, the Moon Goddess [20]

tion is west of the Milky Way, and its Altair star represents Niu Lang. In early autumn, the Milky Way appears dimmer because its brightest part, the galactic core, is less visible. Thus, Zhinu can cross it.

Among the other significant deities in the Jade Emperor's court was the Moon Goddess, Chang'e. She was not always a goddess. Once, she was a stunningly beautiful woman with hair as black as night, skin as white as milk, and cherry-red lips. Her husband was the celebrated archer Hou Yi. At that time, the world had ten suns instead of one, making the Earth too hot for people to survive. Hou Yi shot down nine of the suns, leaving only one, which gave the correct amount of warmth and light.

Wang Mu, the Queen of Heaven, visited him in mid-autumn, rewarding him with the Elixir of Life. "If you drink half of this vial, you will live forever. If you drink it all, you will become a god," she told him.

Hou Yi could not decide what to do with the elixir. What good was it to live forever if his wife would die one day? What good was it to be a god if his wife was still a mortal? He gave the vial with the Elixir of Life to his wife, Chang'e, before going out hunting. "Keep this safe for me until I decide what to do with it," he said.

However, Hou Yi had a student named Peng Meng with a treacherous and conniving heart. He had been with Hou Yi when Wang Mu gave him the elixir. After Hou Yi left for the hunt, Peng Meng burst into his house. Chang'e was playing with her pet rabbit and screamed when she saw the intruder.

"Give me the Elixir of Life!" Peng Meng snarled.

Realizing the darkness of his heart, Chang'e knew she could not let him have it. If he became immortal, he would be a demon. To keep it from Peng Meng, she grabbed the vial and drank it all. Still holding her rabbit, she floated out the window and into the sky. Peng Meng ran off, never to be seen again. That night, Hou Yi came home, and his wife's maid told him what had happened.

Hou Yi ran outside. "Chang'e! Chang'e! Come back to me!" he cried.

He realized the moon was exceptionally bright, and then he saw the shape of the rabbit on the moon. "She's up there! She's the Moon Goddess now."

He called the servants and said, "Quick! Put an altar here in the courtyard and place little cakes and fruit on it! We must honor my wife, who has become a goddess."

From that time until today, the Chinese people gather to celebrate the Mid-Autumn Festival, eating "moon cakes" stuffed with delicacies.

Caishen, the God of Wealth (Zhao Gongming)[80]

Caishen, the god of wealth, was also at one time a human named Zhao Gongming. When the Qin dynasty (221-206 BCE) came to power, he retreated to Mount Zhongnan to cultivate Dao. Once he achieved Dao, he became immortal but did not become the god of money until the Tang dynasty (618-907 CE). Initially, the Jade Emperor made him the Lieutenant Marshal of the Divine Clouds, one of the Five Gods of Pestilence. (They did not send pestilence; they protected people from it.)

In this role, Caishen commanded the clouds to send thunder, lightning, wind, and rain. He oversaw law and order among the people, exacting punishment for the guilty but showing mercy to those who repented. He and his fellow gods healed sicknesses and protected people from epidemics, such as the plague. Once he became the god of money, he helped people build financial fortunes but also policed fair trade and honest business practices.

Some images of Caishen show him riding a tiger. He has a black face and beard and wears an iron crown. He might hold a whip, a sword, or a money bowl. At Spring Festival (Chinese New Year), Chinese people invoke Caishen's blessing as they greet each other with "Gōngxǐ fācái," which literally means, "Congratulations! May you get rich!" At Chinese New Year, married adults give red envelopes with money to children and young, unmarried people. Employers give bonuses in red envelopes to their employees.

A sword, snake, lute, and parasol are symbols of the Four Heavenly Kings who were immediately under the Jade Emperor in Taoist and Buddhist theology. The Four Heavenly Kings guarded the world's four cardinal directions (or, sometimes, the four corners). Artwork of the Four Kings usually shows them wearing full armor, and each holds one of the four objects.

Duowen Tianwang, the "King of News," guards the north. He hears everything and carries an umbrella because he brings rain. Zengchiang Tianwang, the "King of Growth," guards the south and carries a sword. He causes roots to grow and rules the wind. Chiguo Tianwang, the "Upholder of the Kingdom," guards the east. He carries a lute, which he plays to bring people to the "way," or the truth. He protects all the people and animals in the kingdom. Guangmu Tianwang, king of the west, sees everything. He carries a snake, which to the Chinese represents change, renewal, and transformation because the snake can shed its skin.

The Four Heavenly Kings [81]

While defending Heaven and Earth, the Four Heavenly Kings and the Jade Emperor clashed with a cheeky supernatural creature called Sun Wukong, or the Monkey King. A Chinese poet and politician named Wu Cheng'en recorded his exploits in the novel *Journey to the West* in the Ming dynasty (1368–1644 CE). He based it on earlier Chinese folktales and dramas. *Journey to the West* is a fanciful and fictional work, but it is based on the quest of a real monk named Xuanzang (602-664 CE). He traveled to India to study Buddhist scriptures and bring them back to China.[i]

Sun Wukong, the monkey, did not have an ordinary birth. At the top of Mount Huaguo, the "Mountain of Flowers and Fruit," lay a magic stone. When the world was young and the goddess Nuwa was mending the sky, she had dropped one of her colored stones on the mountain. It lay there for millennia, absorbing the rays of the sun and moon and receiving nourishment from yin (Earth) and yang (Heaven). One day, the rock broke open, and inside was a stone egg. As the wind blew on the egg, it hatched, and out popped Sun Wukong, a stone monkey.

At first, the monkey could only move his eyes. When he did, two golden beams shot toward Heaven, alarming the Jade Emperor. "What was that?" the Jade Emperor said, turning to two officers. "Go down to the mountain and find out what is going on! Where did that bright light come from?"

By the time the officers arrived at the mountain, the stone monkey was eating and drinking regular food, losing his stoniness and becoming more like a regular monkey. He had met some wild monkeys on the mountain and was playing with them in a stream. The officers reported to the Jade Emperor what they found. "He doesn't seem to be anything special," they said.

But on the mountain, Sun Wukong, the monkey, was curious about the stream. "Where does this water come from?" he asked.

The other monkeys shrugged. "Somewhere up on the mountain."

"Let's find its source!" Sun Wukong said. He led the other monkeys, following the stream until they reached a waterfall.

"This must be the source of the spring!" the monkeys said. "Whoever goes under the waterfall to the other side will be our next king!"

Sun Wukong took the challenge and bravely plunged into the waterfall. When he did, he entered the "Water Curtain Cave." He called back to the monkeys on the other side of the waterfall: "Everyone, come in here! Look at this cave. It will be our secret palace!"

The monkeys passed through the waterfall and joined him in the cave, pronouncing him their new king.

---

[i] Cheng'en Wu, *Monkey: Journey to the West*, trans. Arthur Waley (Penguin Classics, 1994).

"I'm now 'Handsome Monkey King'!" Sun Wukong laughed.

However, his joy soon faded. His dear friend, an old monkey, died. This was the first time Sun Wukong saw death. "There must be a way to defeat death! I won't rest until I find out," he determined.

Monkey King made a raft and floated down the river, searching for an immortal sage to instruct him in the way of Tao.

A Chinese actor portrays the Monkey King.[39]

After wandering for weeks, the Monkey King finally found a Taoist temple where the sage Puti Zushi taught martial arts and meditation. Puti

Zushi refused to teach the Monkey King, but Sun Wukong dug in his heels and sat at the gate to the temple, waiting. Months later, Puti Zushi asked one of his students, "Is that monkey still out there?"

"Yes, he is."

"Āiyā!" the sage exclaimed, smacking his forehead. "He's not going away. Alright, invite him in. I must say, that monkey has fortitude!"

So, the Monkey King joined the temple, where Puti Zushi taught him Taoist principles and martial arts. Sun Wukong learned to fight with a staff. Through discipline and meditation, he acquired special powers, such as shapeshifting into other animals or objects, and the Cloud Somersault, where a single leap would carry the monkey for miles. Puti Zushi also taught him the secret of immortality through the "seventy-two heavenly methods of transformation."

"Never practice these skills in front of other people just to show off," he warned the monkey. "If you do, other people will aspire to be your students, but they might use the skills for evil. And tell no one who taught you these things. Swear it!"

When the Jade Emperor discovered that the Monkey King had become immortal and learned formidable warrior skills, he gave him a minor position in Heaven's court: Keeper of Horses. "I want him up here, where I can keep an eye on him," the Jade Emperor explained.

Later, after the Monkey King found out that he had Heaven's lowest position, he abandoned Heaven and returned to his mountain cave. Sun Wukong discovered that when he was gone, the Demon King of Confusion had been kidnapping the monkeys from the mountain and enslaving them. The Monkey King killed the demon and rescued the monkeys. Then, he put up a flag advertising himself as "Heaven's Great Sage."

Chapter 3:
Legends From the Silk Road

The Silk Road was not one highway. It was a transportation network linking China to trade with India, Thailand, Indonesia, Central Asia, and eventually Africa, the Middle East, and Europe. The preferred route was by sea, not land. Fleets of ships sailed from the South China Sea into the Indian Ocean, then up the Persian Gulf or the Red Sea. Camel caravans on the Silk Road's land routes traversed China's western deserts and high mountains, extending into India, Afghanistan, and beyond.

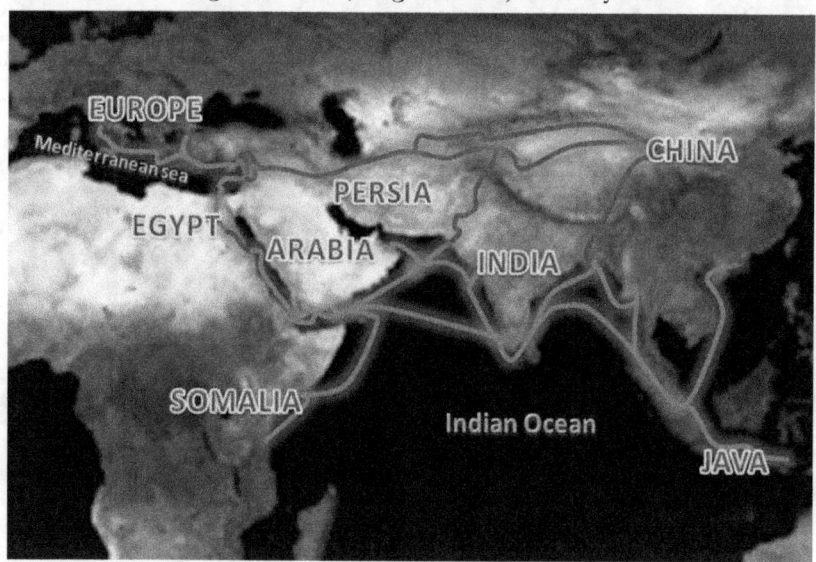

The Silk Road traveled over land and sea.[88]

China exported silk cloth and silk thread to Syria and Lebanon. The Syrians of Damascus used the thread to weave their renowned damask cloth, a luxury item named for their city. The Phoenicians of Tyre also wove silk and dyed it with the coveted purple dye made from murex sea snails. China exported Panax ginseng to Syria, and the Syrians shipped it to Italy. China imported horses and spices from Persia, glass from Egypt, and perfume and precious metals from India. Ships and caravans constantly plied the seas and deserts, transporting goods back and forth. Along with the commodities came new ideas, religions, and innovations. The Silk Road exchanged not only merchandise but also culture.

With such diverse cultural interchange, countless tales emerged of merchants and mythical creatures encountered along the ancient trade routes. Some were renowned historical figures, such as Zhang Qian. Others were legendary heroes who fought bandits and monsters on the intercontinental routes. Their stories symbolize the peril and promise of travel along these treacherous highways and sea routes.

Zhang Qian, known as the "Father of the Silk Road," was an explorer and diplomat during the Han dynasty. His 138 BCE expedition to the Fergana Valley opened the door for China's trade to the West. In his day, China had newfound strength after being led by several powerful emperors. However, the fierce, nomadic Xiongnu tribes made travel through the eastern Eurasian Steppe perilous.

Up to this point, China had small, stocky Mongolian ponies, but news came that "Tianma," or heavenly horses, were being bred in the Fergana Valley (today's southern Kyrgyzstan, eastern Uzbekistan, and northern Tajikistan). "These horses are tall and exceptionally strong!" the reports said. "They can run like the wind, carrying a fully armored man."

Emperor Wudi appointed Zhang Qian to lead an expedition over the Tian Shan Mountain Range (in today's Xinjiang Province). With ninety-nine men, Zhang Qian left the Chinese capital of Chang'an (today's Xi'an). He traveled around the far western end of the Great Wall of China and into the Taklamakan Desert. People gasped when they heard of his planned route. "No one has ever crossed that desert and lived to tell the tale," they murmured.

Sure enough, the Xiongnu captured Zhang Qian's group, enslaving them for over a decade. However, Zhang Qian married a Xiongnu woman, who helped him gain the trust of the Xiongnu chieftain. Finally, Zhang Qian escaped with his guide, his wife, and his son. They pressed on with the desert crossing, then climbed the Tian Shan range with its 24,000-foot mountains. Emperor Wudi's jaw dropped when Zhang Qian stumbled back into China's imperial court thirteen years after he left.

"I thought you were dead!"

"It's all true!" Zhang Qian told Wudi. "There really are heavenly horses! Unfortunately, the people of Fergana refuse to sell them to us."

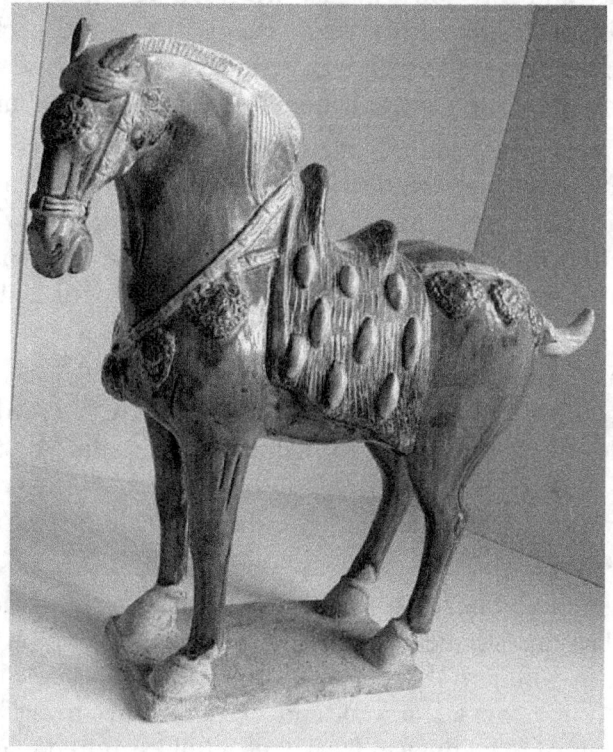

A ceramic Fergana warhorse buried in a Tang dynasty tomb [84]

Wudi frowned. "If the people of Fergana refuse to sell horses to us, we'll take them! And we'll deal with the Xiongnu on the way."

The emperor sent sixty thousand soldiers over the mountains and desert to Fergana, and they captured a herd of horses to bring back to China to breed. They also drove out the Xiongnu.

Once China controlled the Tarim Basin of today's Xinjiang, caravans began traveling from China to the west and northwest, carrying silk to trade for furs, gemstones, and ivory. It opened a whole new world to China. Eventually, the Chinese heard about Rome in the far-distant west. China's silk enchanted the aristocratic Romans, who paid a fortune in gold for the luxurious fabric.

As merchants traveled along the Silk Road, they would stop to rest at desert oases or wayside inns. Travelers from all over paused for a few hours to water their camels or stay the night.

A favorite pastime in these resting places was storytelling. Carpets were a key trade item on the Silk Road, and travelers rested on these as stories were told. (Western China produced knotted wool carpets as early as 1000 BCE, particularly in Khotan on the western edge of the Taklamakan Desert.) Some stories on the Silk Road involved a flying carpet or a magic carpet, which, in Taoism, symbolized spiritual transcendence in the journey toward enlightenment. The Jewish and Arabian versions of the stories describe a rug that transported a man through the air.

China had its own charmed carpets. One Chinese folktale known as **The Enchanted Tapestry** is the story of a widow who spent many years weaving a magical rug that depicted a fantasy world. She pricked her fingers and used her blood for the deep red colors, weeping as she wove her masterpiece. Fairies frequently flew into her house to watch her weave the exquisite rug. When she finally finished weaving, the pictures in the tapestry seemed to come alive. The flowers swayed, and the animals danced.

When the fairies reported back to the gods of Sun Mountain in Tibet, they sent a magic wind to snatch up the rug and fly it to the mountain. The woman sent her three sons to retrieve it. To take back the tapestry, they had to complete a series of perilous and nearly impossible tasks. The two oldest sons thought it was too hard. Then, a sorceress approached them, bribing them with jewels to abandon their quest. They returned to their mother. "We couldn't get the rug, but look! We brought you these jewels!" they said.

Yet, their mother only wanted the tapestry that she had wept and bled over. Meanwhile, the youngest brother was working his way through the tasks set by the gods of the mountain. He had to climb the Mountain of Fire, then cross the Sea of Ice. Finally, he arrived at Sun Mountain to find fairy princesses weaving copies of his mother's rug. Weary from his long journey, he fell asleep and awakened the following morning to find the rug rolled up next to him. He took it home to his mother, who laughed with joy when he walked in with her beloved tapestry. As he crossed the threshold, the scene on the rug transformed into a real paradise where he and his mother lived from that point on.

A highly sought-after commodity on the Silk Road was rare gemstones. Naturally, tales told around the fire revolved around jewels. An ancient Chinese folktale was the "Marquis of Sui's Pearl." The ruler of the Sui state was inspecting his domain when he came across an enormous python in dire straits, dying from a hideous wound. The marquis stopped the bleeding and bandaged the wound. Grateful, the snake circled him three times, then slithered off.

A year later, the marquis was traveling through the same region on an inspection tour. One night, he dreamed the snake was sending him a giant pearl from its crown as a gesture of gratitude for saving its life. He awakened to find a lustrous pearl lying on the pillow next to him. The ruler treasured the precious pearl, which glowed with the brilliance of gratitude.

The Azure Dragon on the Ming dynasty (1889–1912 CE) national flag [85]

Travelers on the Silk Road frequently passed by cemeteries for those who succumbed to harsh conditions, disease, or brutal attacks by bandits. Among the graves, they noticed carvings of mythical creatures, including the Azure Dragon, the Black Tortoise, the Vermilion Bird, and the White Tiger. These creatures were manifestations of the Four Heavenly Kings, representing the four cardinal directions. The ancient Chinese believed these creatures protected the caravans.

The most famous mythical creature to travel the Silk Road was Sun Wukong, the Monkey King, who journeyed to India in search of Buddhahood. As you may remember from chapter two, ***Journey to the West*** describes his mythical adventures, based on the sixteen-year pilgrimage of Xuanzang, a real-life seventh-century monk. Folktales, poetry, and dramas of Xuanzang's journey had circulated for centuries. A central character in the story was Tang Sanzang, who represented Xuanzang. Tang Sanzang, the "Longevity Monk," was found in a river as a baby. He was a reincarnation of the Golden Cicada, a disciple of the Buddha.

The impudent Monkey King was back in Heaven at this point and had been stirring up chaos. The Jade Emperor was at his wits' end. He tried jailing Sun Wukong and even attempted to kill him, but the clever creature always escaped. Finally, the Jade Emperor asked the Buddha for help. The Buddha traveled from his temple in India to meet with the Jade Emperor in

A painting of the monk Xuanzang on his way to India[86]

Heaven. Sun Wukong brazenly leaped between the Buddha and the Jade Emperor.

"I should be the next Jade Emperor!"

A collective gasp arose in Heaven at Sun Wukong's irreverence. The Buddha raised one eyebrow, then turned to the Jade Emperor. "I see what you mean. He's incorrigible."

He reached down and picked up the Monkey King, balancing him on his hand. "I bet you cannot get out of my palm."

The Monkey King laughed and rushed off. He ran to what he thought was the edge of the universe, where he saw five high pillars. "I've reached the end of existence!" Sun Wukong exclaimed. He hopped about, peeing on one pillar and writing graffiti on another: "Sun Wukong is the Great Sage equal to Heaven."

The Monkey King ran back to the Buddha, only to find that what he thought were pillars were the Buddha's fingers. He had never left the Buddha's palm. Yet, at that point, he suddenly did, as the Buddha threw him down to Earth, sending a mountain of rocks to cover him. Only his hands and head stuck out from the bottom of the mountain. Sun Wukong remained imprisoned for five hundred years.

"Stay there until you learn humility and patience!" the Buddha sternly admonished him.

After five centuries, the Monkey King heard that Guanyin was looking for pilgrims to travel west with a monk named Tang Sanzang. Guanyin was a bodhisattva, a person who had achieved enlightenment but delayed entering the transcendent state of nirvana to help others reach Buddhahood. (Guanyin was originally a man in India, but the Chinese later portrayed him as a woman.) She was now helping others on their path and was looking for pilgrims to travel to India with Tang Sanzang to bring Mahayana Buddhist scriptures back to China.

The Monkey King sent Guanyin a message: "I'll happily serve Tang Sanzang on his pilgrimage to Tianzhu (India) if you set me free from this mountain."

Guanyin had heard that the Monkey King was impossible to control. She gave Tang Sanzang a magic golden circlet. "Once the Monkey King puts it on his head, it will never come off. I'll give you a sutra to chant if he is naughty. The circlet will tighten, giving him a dreadful headache. It will remind him of the restraint required in Buddhism."

Guanyin then visited the Monkey King, giving him three hairs. "If you are ever in an impossible situation, use one of

A Song dynasty (960-1279 CE) painting of Guanyin [87]

these hairs," she instructed. "They will transform you into something that will enable you to escape."

The Monkey King set off on the pilgrimage to India with Tang Sanzang. He redeemed himself by faithfully focusing on the task at hand, which was to assist and protect Tang Sanzang. He put into play the martial arts skills that Puti Zushi had taught him centuries earlier. Part of the small group was Zhu Bajie (Pigsy), Sha Wujing (Sand Monk or Sandy), and Bai Long Ma (White Dragon Horse). They served alongside the Monkey King as bodyguards to atone for their past sins.

Pigsy had a pig head and a human body. He overate, and was lazy and easily distracted by pretty women. He once saw the Moon Goddess, Chang'e, and tried to seduce her. Heaven punished him by giving him a pig's head. Tang Sanzang regularly reminded him of the "eight restraints" of Buddhism: don't kill, steal, misbehave sexually, lie, get drunk, or eat after noon. Avoid luxury and mindless entertainment. Despite not being an exemplary Buddhist, Pigsy possessed some impressive powers. He could flip yin and yang (turning cold to hot, day to night), trigger earthquakes, and ride on clouds.

Sandy had once been a general in Heaven until he broke a jade goblet during the Heavenly Peach Festival. Was it an accident, or did he do it on purpose? The Jade Emperor assumed the latter, sentencing him to eight hundred swats with a rod. Then, he sent Sandy to Earth, where he reincarnated as a man-eating monster with a red beard and blue skin who lived in quicksand. He carried a magic rod and wore a necklace of skulls (victims he had eaten). Guanyin converted him to Buddhism, and he became a model disciple, loyal and obedient to Tang Sanzang, as well as kind-hearted and polite toward his fellow pilgrims.

Tang Sanzang rode on the White Dragon Horse, who was the son of the Dragon King of the West Sea. The Dragon King had accidentally burned a precious pearl given by the Jade Emperor and was sentenced to die. Guanyin pleaded for his life and then sent the dragon to the Yingchou Stream, which flowed from Shepan Mountain, to wait for Tang Sanzang.

However, when the monk arrived, the dragon failed to recognize him and ate his white horse in a single gulp. Then, he launched into battle with the Monkey King. Just then, a Tudigong, or earth deity, whispered to the Monkey King, "Guanyin sent the dragon! He's supposed to help Tang Sanzang."

Sun Wukong stopped fighting the dragon, who transformed into the White Dragon Horse that carried the monk on the journey.

Monkey King, White Dragon Horse, Tang Sanzang, Pigsy, and Sandy
in a painting from Beijing's Summer Palace[98]

Sometime later, the Yellow Robe Demon, who lived in Moon Winds Cave, captured Tang Sanzang so he could eat him. The White Dragon Horse tried to save the monk but failed. "Pigsy!" he cried. "Go to Flower Fruit Mountain and get the Monkey King!"

Shortly before this happened, a Cadaver Demon named Lady White Bone tried to capture Tang Sanzang. She wanted to eat the monk, thinking it would make her immortal. The demon transformed into a beautiful princess to deceive Tang Sanzang. However, she did not fool the Monkey King. He smacked the "princess" with his staff. The demon shapeshifted into an old lady and then into an elderly man. Both times, the Monkey King saw through her disguise and finally killed the demon.

Sun Wukong's actions horrified the monk. He did not realize that the princess, the old lady, and the old man were all personifications of a demon. He thought the Monkey King was abusing and killing innocent people, so he banished him from the pilgrimage. Sun Wukong returned to Flower Fruit Mountain and his monkey subjects.

So, when Pigsy rushed to the mountain, begging him to come save Tang Sanzang, the Monkey King frowned. "The monk banished me!"

Pigsy appealed to his vanity. "I know, Monkey King, but he was mistaken. You must rescue him! You're the only one who can! By the way, you'll never believe what that Yellow Robe Demon said about you."

This triggered the Monkey King into action. He flew back to save Tang Sanzang; however, the Yellow Robe Demon blew him away with a fierce gust of wind. But the indomitable Monkey King flew back and continued fighting until he rescued Tang Sanzang from the demon's cave.

Tang Sanzang needed bodyguards because bandits were always a threat on the Silk Road. Demons and other supernatural creatures were constantly on the attack, thinking they could become immortal and superpowerful if they ate the monk. The pilgrims suffered eighty-one tribulations on the journey, but these perils were part of the testing they had to endure to achieve their spiritual goals. As they traveled, Tang Sanzang instructed them in Buddhist teachings and encouraged them to lead virtuous lives.

The Monkey King used several supernatural martial arts tactics when defending the pilgrims. One was the Cloud Somersault, a leap and flip that covered 34,000 miles. To activate this spell, he spoke an incantation, made a special hand sign, clenched his fist, and then shook his body. Sun Wukong also used the Seventy-two Transformations, which allowed him to shapeshift into a variety of animals or objects. It also enabled him to become invisible, change the weather, heal, or teleport.

After a harrowing journey, Tang Sanzang and his group reached India's (real) Vulture Peak, home of the (legendary) Thunderclap Monastery. The pilgrims acquired the sacred scrolls they were seeking and returned safely to China. For his faithful service and stellar defense of the pilgrims, the Monkey King became spiritually enlightened and attained Buddhahood, with the title "Victorious Fighting Buddha." His golden circlet, which tightened when he misbehaved, disappeared.

Chapter 4: Tales of the Lotus Pond

The prince and poet Cao Zhi, who lived in China's Three Kingdoms period (220-280 CE), once said, "Of all the plants in the world, the lotus flower is unique." In his poem "Ode to the Nymph of the Luo River," Cao Zhi compared the goddess to the flower: "She is as luminous as a lotus emerging from clear ripplets."[i]

Sacred lotus [89]

---

[i] Robert Joe Cutter, *The Poetry of Cao Zhi* (De Gruyter, 2021).

Ponds with floating lotus flowers are an integral part of China's landscape. Lotus flowers hold special significance in Chinese legends, as they symbolize purity, enlightenment, and rebirth in both Buddhist and Taoist traditions. The ancient Chinese perceived lotus ponds as transformed realms where divine creatures and enlightened beings lived.

In Chinese legend, **He Xiangu** was a breathtakingly beautiful yet chaste young woman who became one of the Ba Xian—the Eight Immortals of Taoism. As with most Chinese names, the first name "He" was her surname. Her given name, "Xiangu," means "fairy aunt." Artwork of Xiangu often depicts her with a lotus, as her story illustrates the transformational and purifying qualities attributed to the flower.

Who were the Eight Immortals? They were originally human beings who became "Xian," celestial or immortal beings. Together, they fought against evil and injustice. He Xiangu was the only woman, although one of the other immortals, Lan Caihe, was a man who wore women's clothing. The Eight Immortals lived on an island group in the Bohai Sea (the top part of the Yellow Sea off northeastern China's coast). No one else could approach the island because the "weak" water surrounding it could not support a ship's weight. Because they were avid wine drinkers (a common practice in northern China), their nickname was the "Eight Drunken Immortals." They reportedly introduced Zui Quan (Drunken Kung Fu), characterized by swaying, unpredictable, and stumbling moves.

When He Xiangu was born in the Tang dynasty, legend says that a purple mist surrounded the house. Six long hairs hung from the infant's head, a portent of greatness. By the age of four, she had incredible strength, enabling her to lift heavy things.

As a young teen, He Xiangu went up the mountain to pick tea with some other girls. She got distracted while searching for the right leaves, and when she looked up, she could not see her friends. The young girl was walking up the path, looking for her companions, when she saw an ancient man with a long beard, a six-tiered robe, and a tall cap. As she drew closer, she realized he had blue eyes, something she had never seen before. He was Lu Dongbin, a scholar and poet who had lived for 250 years in his human body and was now one of the Immortals.

Lu Dongbin was probably the first teacher of neidan shu (inner alchemy), which focused on extending one's physical life and enabling one's spirit to live eternally. Neidan employed Taoist meditations and other practices to understand the connections between the spiritual, natural, and bodily realms. Lu Dongbin would eventually invite He Xiangu to become one of the Eight Immortals, but first, she needed to prepare herself.

The Eight Immortals crossing the sea. He Xiangu stands at the stern, holding the rudder. Her collar represents the white lotus.⁴⁰

He told her to eat powdered mica (a colored or transparent sparkling mineral that separates into thin leaves), explaining, "If you do this, you will become delicate and light, and on the path to immortality."

He Xiangu followed Lu Dongbin's instructions, which also included being sexually celibate and eating very little food. When she looked at the glistening mica, Xiangu saw celestial flowers—white lotus buds (probably hallucinating due to starvation). She became so thin that many people thought she was a wraith (ghost) even when she was still a mortal.

Following custom, He Xiangu's parents arranged a marriage for her. Yet, on the night of the wedding, she disappeared. She left a note behind, explaining that marriage was an earthly distraction from the destiny the gods had ordained for her. Instead, she said, "I shall listen to the phoenix playing the flute in the moonlight while riding the celestial crane on the journey to immortality."

He Xiangu riding the celestial crane in a sixteenth-century Taoist painting[41]

After receiving instructions in a dream, He Xiangu began eating mother-of-pearl as part of the path to immortality. This enabled her to transcend her physical body and glide effortlessly through the air, over the hills. She gathered herbs on her flying excursions, which she brought home and studied to learn how to use them to heal people. She is associated with the white lotus because it is a symbol of health, harmony, and well-being.

One day during the reign of the Tang dynasty Emperor Zhongzong, He Xiangu flew up to Heaven and became one of the Eight Immortals. Artwork of Xiangu often portrays her as a young, ethereal woman with delicate features and long black hair, holding a lotus flower in her hand.

The Dragon King's Daughter is the story of how a little girl called Longnu (Dragon Girl) became the first female Buddha.

In the Buddhist religion, there is not just one Buddha. Buddhism arrived in China via the Silk Road from India in the first century CE during the Han dynasty. The first Buddha was Siddhartha Gautama, who founded Buddhism in India. The word "Buddha" means "awakened," referring to those who have achieved enlightenment by truly understanding reality and detaching from impermanent things. When they achieve Buddhahood, suffering is extinguished, and they enter the state of nirvana, or perfect freedom. In Buddhism, the lotus flower is a symbol of the transcendence of worldly desires.

The little girl's story is told in the *Lotus Sutra*, the primary scripture for Chinese and other East Asia Buddhists. Longnu's father was Sagara, the Dragon King. He was a naga, half-human and half-serpent. Sagara lived in a palace at the bottom of the ocean and ruled over the rain.

At the tender age of eight, Longnu was renowned for her intelligence, keen memory, and understanding of the lives of people and animals. She memorized lengthy Buddhist mantras using "dharanis," or mnemonics and chants. Longnu could enter deep meditation and understand the dharmas—the Buddha's teachings on how elements of the empirical world connected.

Eager for enlightenment, Longnu reached a state of non-retrogression. This is a stage a Buddhist disciple reaches when they are certain they will continue to progress spiritually into higher levels of existence without backsliding or giving up. It is the point of no return on their journey to Buddhahood. In this stage, Longnu's compassion extended to all people and animals as if they were her children. She was harmonious and merciful to all.

Manjushri was a bodhisattva who embodied transcendent wisdom. The *Lotus Sutra* records that Manjushri was proud of Longnu's progress and spoke about her approvingly when he was asked if anyone could attain Buddhahood quickly:

A silver figure of Manjushri holding a lotus [48]

> "The daughter of the Dragon King has just turned eight. She has deep wisdom and a keen perception of people's activities and motivations. This little girl has mastered the dharanis and understands a storehouse of the Buddha's profound secrets. She has entered into deep meditation and has attained no regression. The blessed child can understand and teach competently and comprehensively."

At that moment, Longnu, the Dragon King's daughter, arrived at Vulture Peak, where the Buddha was. Sariputra, one of the Buddha's chief disciples, scoffed when he saw the little girl:

> "Do you think that in such a short time you have attained the Way? I find this hard to believe! You're a girl! A woman's body is defiled, incapable of receiving the Law. And that's not all! The journey to Buddhahood is extensive. It takes immeasurable time for a person to receive formal instruction and practice good deeds. As a female, five obstacles stand in your way! A woman cannot become a Brahma. She cannot become a Sakra, lord of celestial beings. A woman cannot become a devil king or a sage king. She cannot become a Buddha. So how can you attain Buddhahood so quickly?"

Longnu did not answer Sariputra. She was holding a precious jewel in her hands, worth more than all the treasures on earth. The Dragon King's daughter walked up to the Buddha and gave him the jewel, which he instantly accepted.

Longnu turned to the others. "Did you see him accept my gift without hesitation?"

"Yes! Immediately!" Everyone nodded.

Longnu smiled. "Now, watch me achieve Buddhahood. It will happen even faster!"

Within a second, the Dragon King's daughter transformed into a man. In the blink of an eye, in Longnu's new male form, he performed all the duties of a bodhisattva. He then traveled to the Spotless World of the South (the Pure Land), where he sat on a jeweled lotus and attained enlightenment. He explained and expounded on Buddhist law to people and creatures everywhere. Women, dragons, and animals were all ecstatic that it was indeed possible for them to achieve enlightenment.

Statue of Longnu in Thailand's Hatyai Buddhist Theme Park [48]

Besides her story in the *Lotus Sutra*, Longnu appeared in Chinese folklore, recorded in the *Precious Scroll of Sudhana and Longnu*. In this narrative, Longnu is an acolyte of Guanyin, the Bodhisattva of Compassion, alongside Shancai (Sudhana), also known as "Red Boy." Shancai first appeared in *Journey to the West*, where he was a monster that shot inextinguishable fire from his mouth. He got into a fierce battle with the Monkey King when he tried to eat Tang Sanzang, the monk. The Monkey King asked Longnu's father, the Dragon King, to send rain, but it did not put out Red Boy's fire. Shancai transformed himself into a lookalike of Guanyin to deceive the Monkey King.

When the Monkey King realized the deception, he went to the real Guanyin for help. Hearing the Red Boy had pretended to be her, she was furious. Guanyin extinguished the fire and gave Monkey King a confusion spell to use against Red Boy. After battling the Monkey King and Guanyin, Red Boy finally surrendered and became Guanyin's student.

At this time, the very young Longnu had not yet begun her journey to Buddhahood. Yet, as the daughter of the Dragon King, she had special powers. One day, Red Boy was walking through the mountains when he heard a little girl crying. He looked down and saw a bottle containing a tiny snake.

"Please! Get me out of this bottle!" the snake said.

Red Boy uncorked the bottle and set her free, but then the snake, Longnu, transformed into a dragon.

"Don't eat me!" Red Boy screamed in terror.

"I'm a dragon. We eat people. It's the way of the world," she replied.

"But I just rescued you from the bottle!" Red Boy cried.

"Oh, alright!" Longnu sighed. "Let's have three judges hear your case and decide whether your good deed outweighs nature."

The first judge, the Water Buffalo Star, sided with Longnu. He had been kicked out of Heaven and badly treated by humans, so he had no sympathy for them. The second judge, a Taoist priest, also sided with the dragon. He avoided involvement in earthly matters, believing events should follow their natural course.

The third judge was a little girl who likewise took Longnu's side: "Yes, you can eat Red Boy. You can even eat me! But first, show me how you could fit into that little bottle."

Longnu shapeshifted back into a little snake and slithered into the bottle. The girl instantly plugged the bottle, entrapping Longnu. Then the girl transformed into her true identity, Guanyin.

"Please, I beg you for mercy!" Longnu cried.

"If you want to be saved," Guanyin told her, "you must study enlightenment at the Grotto of the Sounds of the Flood."

And that is how Longnu became a student of Guanyin and began her path to Buddhahood. Ironically, Longnu had to transform into a man to achieve enlightenment. However, Guanyin had been a man in India but shifted into a woman when she came to China after becoming a bodhisattva. (It's possible that the Chinese misinterpreted Indian paintings and sculptures of Guanyin. Men often appeared somewhat androgynous in Indian religious art.)

The Butterfly Lovers, or **Liang Shanbo and Zhu Yingtai**, is among several Chinese folktales that feature the lotus or lotus pond as a motif for spiritual union and eternal love. The lotus pond at Liangzhu Cultural Park in Ningbo, Zhejiang Province, China, commemorates the lovers. Along with the lotus pond, the park also features terraces, pavilions, the Nine Dragon Pool, sculptures of the lovers, and an ornamental bridge symbolizing marriage.

Here's how the story goes.

Zhu Yingtai was the pretty and intelligent daughter of a wealthy father. One day, as a young teen, she marched up to her father and said, "I want to go to school!"

"Yingtai, my darling, only boys go to school. You've already learned how to read and write here at home."

"I know, Baba, but it isn't the same! The boys are studying the Chinese masters, learning philosophy and the classics. I want to do the same!"

"My sweet daughter, they won't let a girl into the school."

"I'll disguise myself as a boy. And my maid will come with me, also in disguise."

After her father relented, Yingtai and her maid headed to the boarding school, dressed as boys. While traveling, Yingtai met a handsome boy named Liang Shanbo, who was on his way to the same school. They quickly became friends, and Shanbo considered Yingtai his brother. However, Yingtai soon fell in love with Shanbo.

After three years, Yingtai's father sent a message telling her to return home, as he had arranged a marriage for her. However, Yingtai was deeply in love with Shanbo, who still did not know she was a girl. Shambo accompanied Yingtai on the first eighteen miles of her journey home, but despite several hints, he did not guess Yingtai's true gender.

Before the wedding, however, Shanbo traveled to Yingtai's village to visit her. He was shocked to discover that his "brother" was a girl! He now realized that he was in love with her, and they vowed to be together forever.

Shanbo approached Yingtai's father, asking for her hand in marriage.

"I have already betrothed her to another," the father explained. "My family will lose face if we break the agreement."

Shanbo stumbled off, weeping. He could not bear to face life without his beloved Yingtai. He refused to eat and withered away. "I'm going to die soon," he told his servant. "Bury me by the side of the road where Yingtai will pass by on her wedding day."

Finally, the fortune teller picked out an auspicious day for the marriage. The women clothed Yingtai in a scarlet dress and draped her with jewels. Her friends and family escorted her toward her fiancé's village with much fanfare—music, firecrackers, and red banners proclaiming good fortune over the marriage. Suddenly, a wild windstorm tore down the road, forcing the wedding party to take shelter. Yingtai looked out from her decorated sedan chair, realizing they had stopped by Shanbo's grave.

The bride stepped down from her palanquin and approached her lover's burial place. Suddenly, a clap of thunder rang out, and the grave opened. Without hesitation, Yingtai threw herself into the gaping hole. At that moment, the storm stopped, and the sun came out. Yingtai's family approached the grave but could not see her. Then, to their astonishment, two butterflies fluttered out of the opening in the ground, spiraling upward until they disappeared into the sky.

The Butterfly Lover's sculpture at Liangzhu Culture Park"

Chapter 5: The Gift of the Dragon

Even today, the dragon holds a pivotal role in Chinese culture. While Westerners typically consider dragons to be fire-breathing, malevolent creatures, the Chinese believe dragons are complex. They can sometimes create chaos, but they can also be benevolent, bringing favorable fortune and strength. The Chinese dragon is associated with water and weather, making it a revered figure in agricultural societies for its rain-making ability, which brings prosperity. In ancient times, the dragon was closely associated with the emperor. Today, it embodies the Chinese spirit.

Every year, the Chinese celebrate the **Dragon Boat Festival** (Duanwu Jie) in May or June. They eat sticky rice dumplings, race dragon boats, and pray for good luck. The Chinese believe that the fifth day of the fifth month (Double Fifth Day) is especially unlucky. On this day, people are likely to be stung by scorpions, bitten by snakes, or stricken with sickness. Dragon Boat races counteract evil.

Dragon boats are long, narrow, uncovered boats propelled by a team of paddlers. The boats have a dragon head at the bow and a dragon tail curling up from the stern. Brightly painted reptilian scales cover the hull.

Three Chinese stories, loosely based on historical events, connect to the Dragon Boat Festival. One is the story of **Qu Yuan**, a highly respected poet and government official in the Warring States period (475-221 BCE). He was part of the Chu royal family and served as an advisor to King Huai. However, he had rivals in court. When facing an invasion by King Zhao of Qin, Qu Yuan proposed a strategic alliance with other Chinese states. His enemies at court slandered him, insinuating that he had ulterior motives for allying with other states. King Huai believed them and exiled Qu Yuan. Failure to heed Qu Yuan's warnings brought disaster. King Zhao of Qin captured King Huai, and he died in captivity.

Qu Yuan mourned his king and, in his poetry, lamented the Chu state's decline. He grew frail and ultimately committed suicide by throwing himself into the Miluo River. When the local people saw him fall into the river, they jumped into their boats and rowed to rescue him. After realizing they were too late, they threw sticky rice dumplings wrapped in bamboo leaves into the water as an offering to the river spirits. (Qu Yuan wrote about offering sacrifices to the water spirits in his lifetime.)

A Qing dynasty cloisonne enamel depiction of the Dragon Boat Festival "

Another Dragon Boat story connects to the tale of **Xi Shi**, one of the "Four Great Beauties" in ancient China. Xi Shi lived in eastern China during the late Spring and Autumn period. Legend says that when she leaned over a lotus pond, the carp stopped swimming in awe of her stunning beauty. The entire idiom is, "Beauty that makes the fish sink, and flying geese fall to the ground. The moon blushes, and flowers close their blooms."

King Goujian of the state of Yue gifted Xi Shi as a concubine to King Fuchai of Wu. Goujian had suffered a defeat at the hands of Fuchai in battle and was forced to pay tribute. The "gift" was a "sexpionage" operation. Xi Shi and another lovely lady were actually secret agents. The two charming young women so enchanted King Fuchai that he neglected affairs of state to spend all his time with them, especially Xi Shi.

King Fuchai built the "Palace of Beautiful Women" in a rural setting and spent more time there than in his capital. He took Xi Shi riding around in his carriage and followed her advice. When she told him she disliked his chief military advisor, the king handed a sword to General Wu Zixu, ordering his loyal military commander to kill himself. Then, he ordered his servants to throw Wu's body into the river.

With General Wu gone and King Fuchai ignoring the safety of his realm, King Goujian swept in with his army, utterly overwhelming Fuchai's forces. In remorse, Fuchai committed suicide. The people of eastern China began worshiping General Wu as the "God of the Waves." They considered him responsible for the Qiantang River's tidal bore (a surge during high tide), the largest in the world. Eventually, the Dragon Boat Festival in eastern China became associated with General Wu.

A third tale connected to the Dragon Boat Festival was about a girl named **Cao E** who lived in eastern China several hundred years after General Wu. When Cao E was thirteen, her father fell into the river while paddling a dragon boat in the races. The people searched for seventeen days but could not find his body. Finally, Cao E waded into the river and disappeared.

Five days later, her body resurfaced, holding her father's body. The local people considered this an astounding example of filial piety—respect and love for one's parents and ancestors. They immediately began worshiping her and built a temple in Cao E's honor. Today, in Shaoxing, Zhejiang Province, the local people hold a memorial service at her temple during the Dragon Boat Festival.

A silk Kesi tapestry of a dragon [46]

The tale of **Yu and the Dragon Gate** takes us back to when Gonggong, the water god, banged his head on one of the four pillars that held up the sky and unleashed the Great Flood. This version of China's flood story happened at the beginning of the Xia dynasty (2070–1600 BCE), China's first dynasty, before the development of writing. In this version, the flood was localized in the Yellow River Valley, the cradle of Chinese civilization. The floodwaters continued for years, destroying the cities and farms along the Yellow and Yangtze rivers.

Historians once thought the Great Chinese Flood and even the Xia dynasty were mythical. However, recent archaeological evidence suggests a significant, prolonged flood occurred in the Yellow River Valley near the beginning of the Xia dynasty.[i] An earthquake caused a landslide, which dammed the Yellow River where it flows from the Tibetan Plateau and through the Jishi Gorge. Because of this discovery, some historians moved the beginning date of the Xia dynasty to 1900 BCE. This is also when the Yellow River Basin transitioned from a Neolithic culture to a Bronze Age civilization.

The Han dynasty historian Sima Qian recorded the myth, saying the Yellow and Yangtze rivers and their tributaries all flooded for two generations.

> "King Yao moaned, 'Like endless boiling water, the flood is pouring forth destruction. Boundless and overwhelming, it overtops hills and mountains. Rising and ever rising, it threatens the very heavens. How the people must be groaning and suffering!'"[ii]

King Yao sought advice from the "Four Mountains" (perhaps four major gods or the four pillars that held up the sky). They told him to make his distant cousin Gun his flood control manager. Yet, Yao's sorcerer sniffed, "This will not end well!"

King Yao had no other option, so he appointed Gun to deal with the flooding. Gun put the people to work building dams to control the flood. Yet the surging water was so strong that it broke the dams. After nine years of failure, Gun stole some divine soil called "Xirang" from Heaven. When he built dams with this material, it expanded when touched by water, successfully controlling the flooding. Everyone breathed a sigh of relief.

However, the god of Heaven found out that Gun had stolen his dirt. "Kill him!" he ordered Zhurong, the god of fire. "Get my dirt back!"

So, Zhurong killed Gun, retrieved the Xirang, and brought it back to Heaven. Immediately, disaster struck the Yellow River Basin again. The

---

[i] Qinglong Wu, et al., "Outburst Flood at 1920 BCE Supports Historicity of China's Great Flood and the Xia Dynasty," *Science* 353, no. 6299 (2016): 579-582, https://www.science.org/doi/10.1126/science.aaf0842

[ii] Qian, Sima. "Shiji, Records of the Grand Scribe," *China Knowledge: An Encyclopaedia on Chinese History and Literature*, accessed March 13, 2025, http://www.chinaknowledge.de/Literature/Historiography/shiji.html

dams collapsed, and the floodwaters submerged the land. The people laid Gun to rest in a tomb, but his body did not decompose. Three years later, Yu emerged from his belly as a dragon. By this time, King Yao had resigned in disgrace. The new ruler, King Shun, ordered Yu to finish the work his father had started. Instead of building dams, Yu opted to create channels to drain the water into the East China Sea. He used a channel-digging dragon and a mud-hauling turtle to assist his engineering efforts.

Jishi Mountain stood in the way, so he tunneled through it. Then, he encountered another mountain, which he split in two, calling the gap "Longmen" or "Dragon Gate." As the river flowed through the Dragon Gate, it created a spectacular waterfall. Yu continued to build his channels to drain the water from the Yellow River Basin, splitting or tunneling through more mountains. After thirteen years, Yu successfully drained the excess river water into the East China Sea. With the floodwaters gone, the people rejoiced, and King Shun made Yu his successor. Yu "the Great" began the Xia dynasty and ruled for forty-five years.

A silk and metallic thread dragon tapestry on a Ming dynasty imperial court robe [e]

Dragons guarded Yu's **Longmen (Dragon Gate)**. Carp would try to jump up the steep waterfall. If they could make it through the Dragon Gate without being eaten by dragons or eagles, they would transform into a dragon. The pounding water, jagged rocks, birds of prey, and dragons stopped most fish. Yet, some carp pressed on, determined to reach the top and become dragons.

A playful little carp lived in a lake near the bottom of the Dragon Gate. One day, his grandfather called him over:

"Xiao Yu, do you see that stream flowing into our lake? It passes over multiple waterfalls before reaching here. If you swim up that stream and jump up the waterfalls, you will reach the highest waterfall. It is nearly impossible for a fish to climb. Yet, if you conquer your fear, survive being caught by foxes or birds, and jump to the top of the falls, you will transform into a dragon!"

"A dragon!" the little carp breathed. "I'm going to try!"

Xiao Yu swam up the stream, jumping over the waterfalls, until he reached the bottom of the Dragon Gate. All he could see was mist at the top of the cleft from which water cascaded down. Many other fish were trying to leap up the waterfall, but the swift current pushed them down, or birds of prey caught them. Xiao Yu leaped from ledge to ledge up the falls, staying close to the falling water where the eagles and hawks could not catch him.

Finally, he reached the top, where a dragon guarded the gate. "Don't even think about getting through the gate," the dragon laughed. "You're just a little fish, not worthy of becoming a dragon."

Xiao Yu smiled. "I might be a little fish, but are you really a dragon? You can't even fly!"

"What do you mean? I most certainly can fly!" the dragon huffed.

"Show me!" Xiao Yu challenged.

The angry dragon spread its wings and flew up into the sky, leaving the gate unguarded. Xiao Yu flicked his tail and passed through the gate. Suddenly, he started transforming into a dragon. The dragon guard flew back and said, "Well, I see you tricked me! Yet, I'm happy for you. You showed ingenuity and bravery! You deserve to be a dragon."

Even today, the Chinese idiom "Lǐyú lóngmén" or "Carp jumps the Dragon Gate" means to take a sudden leap forward in circumstances. Specifically, it was used for students who passed the imperial civil service examinations, providing an opportunity for boys from lower- or middle-class families to become government employees.

The guardian dragon (top) and Xiao Yu (bottom) as a new little dragon [48]

Our last dragon story is the **Monkey King and the Dragon King**. This tale takes place before Sun Wukong, the Monkey King, went on the pilgrimage to India. He had briefly served in Heaven until he found out he had the lowest job. So, he returned to Earth and his monkeys, just in time to rescue them from the Demon King of Confusion. To ensure his monkeys would not be enslaved again, Sun Wukong stole weapons from a nearby country to arm his band. Yet, he could not find a suitable weapon to arm himself. Then, Sun Wukong heard that Ao Guang, the Dragon King of the East Sea, had a magnificent collection of weapons.

Ao Guang was a chaos-causing dragon, bringing hurricanes and droughts and disregarding the Jade Emperor. The people offered lavish sacrifices to keep the dragon from wreaking havoc. One day, a seven-year-old divine creature named Nezha took a bath in Jiuwan Stream. His movements sent shockwaves through the underwater aquifer, and the tremors even disturbed Ao Guang in his palace beneath the sea.

Irritated, the Dragon King sent Li Gen, a nature spirit, to find out what was happening, but Nezha killed him. When the Dragon King received this news, his son, Ao Bing, volunteered to avenge Li Gen's death. However, Nezha killed Ao Bing too.

"Enough is enough!" the Dragon King snarled. "I'm going to go see that youngster's father!"

Nezha's father was Li Jing, the Pagoda-bearing Heavenly King. His pagoda could capture any demon or god, and he was a canny military strategist who enabled China to defeat its enemies. When the Dragon King arrived at Li Jing's court, Nezha confessed to his crime. "Yes, I killed your son. I pulled out his tendons to make a belt for my father. Here they are. You can have them."

The Dragon King held his son's tendons in his hand, smoldering. "Li Jing! You must sacrifice yourself to atone for your son's sin!" he demanded. Yet, Li Jing refused.

The Dragon King stormed out, exclaiming, "I'm filing a complaint with the Jade Emperor!" He flew up to Heaven, now embarrassed that he had never offered sacrifices to the Jade Emperor. Nezha also flew up, arriving at Heaven's gates at the same time as the Dragon King. Nezha ambushed and thrashed him, ripping his scales from his body. He forced the Dragon King to shapeshift into a small snake and carried him back to Earth.

The Dragon King struggles with Nezha. [40]

Ao Guang transformed back into a dragon, vowing to round up the other dragon kings and wreak vengeance. When the four dragon kings captured Nezha's parents, Nezha panicked. "Leave them alone!" he pleaded. "I'll give you my internal organs if you release them!"

The Dragon King agreed to the exchange and flew back to Heaven with the intestines as an offering to the Jade Emperor. Sometime later, Sun Wukong, the Monkey King, arrived at the Dragon King's undersea palace, in need of a special weapon. The Dragon King told his guards to send him away, but Sun Wukong pushed his way in.

"Sir!" he said to the Dragon King, "I'm a king, just like you! I would like you to give me a weapon."

The Dragon King furrowed his brow. "Now I know who you are! You studied under Puti Zushi! I have heard that you have exceptional powers. You even served in Heaven as the Jade Emperor's Keeper of Horses."

"Yes," the Monkey King nodded modestly. "But now I'm living on Earth again. I need to protect my monkeys from the demons. Can you help me?"

The Dragon King ordered his servants to bring out an array of weapons. Yet, none was powerful enough for Sun Wukong. Then, the Dragon King's wife spoke up. "What about the Ruyi Jingu Bang?"

The Ruyi Jingu Bang was an iron rod with gold rings on each end that magically expanded or shrank. Yu the Great had used it to measure the water during his flood management campaign.

The Dragon King seemed puzzled by his wife's suggestion. "It's a tool, not a weapon!"

"Yes, but it's been glowing recently," she explained. "I believe it's trying to communicate something to us."

When the Monkey King came close to the rod, the Ruyi Jingu Bang glowed brightly. When he reached out to touch it, it shrank down so he could hold it like a staff.

The Dragon King nodded. "This is the weapon meant for you!"

An actor portraying Sun Wukong with his magic staff in the Beijing Opera[50]

When he heard about this, the Jade Emperor erupted in rage. "What was the Dragon King thinking, giving Sun Wukong the Ruyi Jingu Bang? We will have no end of trouble!"

The Jade Emperor sent his warriors to capture the Monkey King. However, with the supernatural skills taught him by Puti Zushi and his magical Ruyi Jingu Bang staff, the Monkey King fought off all the celestial soldiers.

"Baozha ba! (Blast it!)" the Jade Emperor swore. "All right!" he said in exasperation. "Politely invite him back up here. Make him the guardian of the Celestial Peach Orchard. We need to keep a close eye on that troublemaker."

Heaven's peach trees only produced fruit every few thousand years, but eating the fruit gave supernatural powers. Sun Wukong helped himself to whatever peaches were ripe. After some time, Wang Mu, the Jade

Emperor's wife, was planning her celestial peach banquet and sent her fairies to collect peaches for her guests. When the fairies discovered the Monkey King had eaten most of the peaches, they sucked air through their teeth in annoyance. "You stupid monkey! What is our lady going to serve her guests? You are definitely *not* invited to the banquet!"

"What?" laughed the Monkey King. "I thought I was the guest of honor! After all, I am Heaven's Great Sage!"

The fairies giggled. "To whom do you teach your wisdom? Everyone knows you're just the peach tree gardener!"

Deeply hurt, Sun Wukong sneaked into the banquet hall and stole some wine, then wandered around Heaven, creating mayhem until the Buddha finally imprisoned him under a mountain for five hundred years.

Chapter 6:
Bamboo and Its Significance

Bamboo is so deeply embedded in China's culture that another name for the country is Zhúzi Wángguó, or the Bamboo Kingdom. The largest member of the grass family, bamboo symbolizes virtue, resilience, integrity, and longevity. Bamboo can be a metaphor for a *jūnzǐ*, or a person of noble character, modesty, and flexibility. Because the wind bends bamboo but does not break it, the Chinese consider bamboo an example of standing firm when faced with fierce adversity.

While bamboo features prominently in Chinese artwork, architecture, mythology, and folklore, the Chinese appreciate its practical uses. Before inventing paper, the Chinese wrote on bamboo slips. Even today, they build rafts, cottages, and scaffolding from bamboo canes and weave baskets and chair seats from them. In the heat of summer, the Chinese enjoy sleeping on bamboo mats placed on their beds. The mats circulate air, keeping one cool.

The Chinese brew bamboo leaves for tea and wrap them around sticky rice for steamed dumplings. Young, tender bamboo shoots are a favorite food for people and animals. China's national animal, the giant panda, eats mostly bamboo—up to eighty pounds a day. Chinese musical instruments made from bamboo include the *dizi,* or side-blown flute, and the *xiao,* or end-blown flute. China's earliest firecrackers were hollow bamboo cane stuffed with gunpowder.

Several Chinese idioms center on bamboo. "Xiōng yǒu hang zhú" means "You must picture bamboo in your heart before you can paint it." The saying conveys the idea that one must carefully think out a plan before acting. "Pò zhú zhī shì" translates to "enough force to smash bamboo," meaning irresistible power. "Zhú lán dǎ shuǐ" translates to "drawing water with a bamboo basket," meaning wasted effort, because bamboo baskets leak like sieves.

The story of the **Humble Farmer and the Magical Bamboo Stalk** highlights not only how bamboo brings wealth and good luck but also teaches the values of gratitude, humility, and perseverance. In ancient times, at the base of the emerald hills, sat a village, the home of a diligent farmer named Wei. He grew rice and wheat, toiling hard every day. Despite his efforts, Wei struggled to feed his family and provide for their needs.

Yuan dynasty (1271-1368) ink painting[61]

His neighbors whispered, "That Wei! Our farms are all doing well, but he never seems to accomplish much."

Farmer Wei felt discouraged that his family was still deep in poverty. He had to contend with the whims of nature, like droughts, hailstorms, and savage windstorms that destroyed his crops. Finally, in the depths of despair, Wei wandered into the forest, ready to end it all. However, he encountered a hermit.

"Why are you here in the woods?" the hermit asked.

"I'm a failure!" Wei answered. "I am diligently working on my farm, but I cannot succeed. Can you give me a reason not to end my life?"

The hermit pointed to two plants. "What are these?"

"This one is a fern, and that one is bamboo," Wei answered.

The hermit nodded. "Which plant grows quickly?"

"The fern grows faster. Bamboo takes a long time to grow."

"That's right," answered the hermit. "Both the fern and the bamboo grow next to each other here in the forest and get the same amount of sun, nutrients, and rain. Yet, the young fern grows faster. However, later the bamboo catches up and grows ten times as tall as the fern. Do you know why?"

"Well, no," Wei answered. "I've never thought about it."

"Go back to your farm and your family," the hermit told him. "The answer will come soon."

Wei returned home and resumed farming. One day, in a neglected area of his property, he found an intriguing bamboo shoot that seemed to glisten with light. He carefully dug it up and transplanted it near his house. He meticulously fertilized and watered the glowing bamboo, but it did not seem to grow. Wei felt a kinship with the bamboo shoot. Months passed, and then years, but the bamboo was still a sapling.

His neighbors berated him. "Wei, why are you wasting so much energy on that little bamboo? It will never amount to anything. Stop your foolish dreams!"

Wei's wife consoled him. "Just ignore them, Wei. You're doing your best." Secretly, however, she worried about their finances.

Wei continued caring for his glistening bamboo shoot with unwavering faith. "Everyone thinks I'm mad, yet I believe I'm investing in this plant's hidden potential," he said.

In the fifth year, Wei emerged from his house one morning, stretching and yawning. He glanced at his bamboo shoot. "Wa!" he exclaimed. "Little bamboo! You are much taller this morning than you were yesterday!"

In the following weeks, his bamboo grew at an incredible speed. It rose another foot every hour. Within six weeks, it grew eighty feet high.

The villagers gathered around, their mouths gaping in shock. "Zhēn de ma? (Could it really be?) What kind of magic is this?"

Wei hurried into the forest, looking for the hermit. When he found him, he told him the story, and the hermit smiled and nodded.

"Was it magic?" Wei asked.

"Perhaps a little magic," the hermit said with a twinkle in his eye. "But it is also the payment for your years of continued faith, hard work, and patience. Not everything comes to us quickly. Sometimes, we must invest time and energy for many seasons before we see the fruit of our labor. All those years that you were watering and tending your bamboo shoot, its roots were growing under the ground. You couldn't see them, but they were laying the foundation for a glorious plant. The bamboo needed that root system to support the huge plant it would become."

Qing dynasty (1644-1912) ink and color on a silk painting of birds, bamboo, and camellias [52]

The **Devoted Dog's Bamboo Grave** is a tale of two brothers, Zhang Lan and Zhang Qin. When their parents died, Zhang Lan claimed entitlement to the house and most of the family's farmland, as he was the oldest. He also took the ox and chickens. Zhang Qin got only a small hut to live in, a tiny section of the farm, and the family dog.

Qin sat on a stool in front of his shack, scratching his dog on the head. "It's just you and me, Gǒu. Yet, I'm sure we'll succeed with teamwork and hard labor."

Lan was uninterested in strenuous work. He drank all the rice wine left in the house, then started eating the chickens. After eating all the hens, he had no source of eggs. He forgot to feed and water the ox enough to keep it strong. When he tried to plow the fields with it, the ox balked and refused to pull. Lan beat the animal mercilessly, but the ox kicked him.

"You stupid beast! Now you're my supper!" Lan yelled. He killed the ox and ate it.

When he sobered up the next morning, Lan realized he had no way to plow his fields and no chickens to lay eggs. What would he eat now? He walked over to his brother's hut.

"How are things going for you, Qin?"

"Well, it's not been easy," Qin said. "However, I taught the dog how to pull a plow! We don't have much land, but we've been working hard and growing vegetables. We have enough to eat and even a little to sell at the market so we can buy meat now and then."

"Wa! You taught the dog how to pull the plow? That's brilliant! Let me borrow Gǒu for a few days. My ox died, and I need him to plow my land."

Qin hesitated, knowing his brother was unkind to animals. Yet, he knew Lan needed to eat. "Okay, you can have him for a few days. But you must give him plenty to eat and drink and treat him well."

Lan took the dog to his land and put the plow harness on him. But Gǒu stiffened and refused to cooperate.

"Pull the plow, you stupid dog!" Lan yelled.

Lan kicked and beat the dog, but Gǒu would not pull the plow. Finally, Lan killed the dog and dropped its dead body in front of Qin's shack.

Weeping, Qin stroked Gǒu's head. He could not bear the thought of losing his companion. Qin buried his beloved dog in the corner of his garden.

Weeks later, Qin was surprised to see bamboo shoots springing out of the ground from the dog's grave. They quickly grew into a grove, giving shade for Qin to rest in after laboring on his small plot of land. One day during midday nap time, Qin was dozing under the bamboo. Plink! Something hit him on the head. He sat up, rubbing his head.

"Shénme? (What?)"

Plink! Plunk! Two more things hit his head. He looked down and saw three gold coins. Where did they come from? Qin leaped out of the way as a shower of coins fell from the bamboo. Gold coins covered the dog's grave.

"Oh, Gǒu! You good dog! Did you send these to me? Xièxiè! (Thank you!)"

Qin picked up the coins and poured them into a bag. He had enough money to buy a large farm and build a grand house. When Lan heard of his brother's good fortune, he came by to visit.

"Do you see that bamboo, Lan? It grew from Gǒu's grave. Gold coins are still falling from the bamboo!" Qin said.

Lan pretended to be happy about Qin's new wealth but secretly planned to steal the bamboo. "I'll plant it on my land and reap the gold!"

Lan ripped some of the bamboo from the ground, but as he did, dog excrement sprayed over him. "Āiyā!" he cursed. In a fit of anger, Lan broke the canes he had pulled up and stalked off.

Qin woke up the next morning to find the broken bamboo. He wept and raged yet gathered up the broken canes. "I'll weave a basket with these."

To his surprise, Qin discovered that coins filled the basket each night. Lan heard about the magical bamboo basket and asked to borrow it. "I need some money for my farm! It is your fraternal duty to help me."

Qin gave the basket to Lan, who hurried home with it. However, when he peeked into the basket the next morning, instead of coins, hissing snakes writhed inside it. He ran out of the house screaming and never bothered Qin again.

Bamboo and Turtle is a story about a twelve-year-old boy named Zhúzǐ (Bamboo), whose father was the keeper of the Sacred Tombs at Nanjing. Royal family members and other dignitaries were buried there. Bamboo watched with excitement one day as men carried ten sedan chairs with red velvet cushions. In them rode a group of the royal family visiting the tomb. Bamboo wanted to follow the procession as the imperial family moved through the area.

Qing dynasty painting of a dog and bamboo [55]

"Bamboo! Come back now! They'll think you're a beggar if you tag after them," his father sternly admonished him.

"Yes, Baba." Bamboo stood quietly in front of his house as the grand procession passed by.

Then, something caught his eye. The group had visited a small temple near his house, and the iron gate stood open. Many times, Bamboo had stood at the iron gate peering in at the temple. He could see into the temple's dark room. A pillar covered with inscriptions rested on the back of a giant stone turtle.

He was curious about the turtle and had asked his father, "Baba, why do they have a turtle in that temple? Why not some other animal, like a tiger?"

"It's just the custom," his father answered.

Now, Bamboo looked over his shoulder. His father had gone inside the house. Bamboo dashed over to the temple and hurried through the gate, into the courtyard, and through the temple door. He tripped and fell on its threshold and lay there, catching his breath, noticing the layer of dust on the floor. Then, he heard a noise, so he crawled under the stone turtle to hide.

"Careful!" rumbled a voice above him. "You're stirring up the dust! I'll be choking soon!"

It was the turtle's voice!

"I didn't know you were alive," Bamboo said in a quivering voice.

"There, there. Don't tremble so. But stop kicking up the dust!"

"I meant no harm," said Bamboo. "I've always wanted to see you."

"You wanted to see me?" Turtle chuckled. "Most people just want to read the inscriptions on the pillar resting on my back. The writing is all about emperors from the past. Yet, they barely look at me, and my father was one of the Four Benevolent Animals who assisted Pangu at the beginning of the world."

Bamboo gasped. "Your father was the Black Warrior of the North?"

"Well, my grandfather."

Bamboo's eyes opened wide in wonder.

"Quick!" Turtle commanded. "Run and close that gate, then come back. If your father notices it is open, he'll lock the gate. I want to tell you something when you get back."

Bamboo hurried out to the courtyard and swung the heavy gate closed. When he came back into the temple, Turtle remarked, "I'm weary of holding up this pillar for so many years. Yes, I know it is an honorable task, but my back hurts. Now that the gate is unlocked, I can escape."

"Oh, no!" Bamboo worried. "If you leave, the authorities will blame my father for leaving the gate unlocked. They'll cut off his head!"

"Don't worry! After I get outside the gate, sneak into your house and get your father's keys. Lock the gate, then put the keys back in place," Turtle instructed. "No one will know what happened. I'm too heavy for anyone to carry. They'll think it was the gods at work. This little temple will become famous!"

Bamboo began to weep.

"Why are you crying?" asked Turtle.

"I don't want you to go!" cried Bamboo.

"Then, come with me! We'll explore the world together!"

Bamboo looked at the heavy pillar resting on Turtle's back. "How will you get that off? It's too high to fit through the door."

"I've thought that through," said Turtle. "When I walk through the door, the pillar will hit the lintel, then slide off my back and onto the floor."

However, the escape did not go as planned. Instead of sliding neatly off Turtle's back, the pillar fell backward and smashed into pieces. Bamboo held his breath, terrified that his father would hear the commotion. Several minutes passed, and nothing happened. His father must be on the other side of the tombs, seeing the royal family off.

Turtle lumbered out of the gate, and Bamboo rushed home, grabbed the keys, and hurried back. He locked the gate, put the keys back in the house, and caught up with Turtle. Bamboo trembled with excitement. He had never been on an adventure.

"Where are we going?" he asked Turtle.

"To the place where my grandfather, the Black Warrior of the North, and the other benevolent creatures helped Pangu form the world."

"How far away is it?" Bamboo asked. "You can't walk very fast."

"Oh, we're not walking. We're flying!" Turtle laughed. "Hop on my back. We're traveling to the beginning of the world!"

Once Bamboo climbed up on Turtle's back, they rose in the air and flew faster than Bamboo thought possible. He looked down to see forests, villages, cities, and high mountains. Finally, Turtle flew to the ground. "Here we are! My friends will be here soon—Dragon and Phoenix. They were with my grandfather at the beginning of the world."

Just then, Bamboo heard flapping wings. It was a gigantic dragon!

"Ha ha, Dragon! I got here first. And you thought you could fly faster!"

Minutes later, the Phoenix bird flew in. Bamboo looked on in wonder as the creatures laughed, feasted, and shared stories. As night drew near, Turtle looked at Bamboo.

"It's time for me to go. I need to get Bamboo home before his father thinks he is lost," Turtle said.

Dragon gave Bamboo one of his scales as a memento, which turned to gold when it touched Bamboo's hand. Phoenix gave one of his fiery red feathers. Bamboo climbed onto Turtle's back, and they flew off through the clouds.

Yet suddenly, Bamboo felt himself slipping from Turtle's back. He screamed, realizing he was falling through the air. He saw a stand of tall bamboo below him and grabbed at the leaves to break his fall.

The next thing he knew, he felt his father shaking him, calling his name.

"Bamboo! Come out from under that turtle! How did you even get in here?"

Bamboo looked around. He was back in the temple, under the stone turtle. "Didn't I die?"

His father cocked his head. "You're very much alive, it's time for dinner, and you are covered with dust. Hurry home and clean yourself up! I need to lock this temple."

Turtle holding pillar at Prince Xiao Xiu's grave, 518 BCE[54]

Chapter 7: Phoenix Legends

Mythology in both the East and West featured the phoenix, called Fènghuáng in China. The Chinese believed that this mythical bird was involved with Heaven's primordial forces at the time of creation. It represented fidelity, justice, grace, and kindness. In the Western version, the phoenix passes through cycles of dying, only to be reborn from its own ashes. However, the Chinese perceived Fènghuáng as immortal, first appearing at the creation of the world. A Fènghuáng appeared when civilization was harmonious and prosperous but vanished in times of dissension and violence.

Even in the Neolithic era, the phoenix was a key element of Chinese culture. A shell mound in Hunan Province on the Yuan River, known as the Gaomiao archaeological site, dates to approximately 5000 BCE and features pottery with a phoenix motif. The ancient people of the Gaomiao culture were hunters, fishers, and rice farmers who were the first to develop white pottery on which they painted images, including Fènghuáng. The phoenix ceramics were unearthed in an area with an altar and a sacrifice pit, showing Fènghuáng had spiritual significance.

Artwork with the phoenix and dragon together first appeared in the Yangshao culture (5000-3000 BCE) in Shaanxi Province near Xi'an. The dragon and phoenix motif became highly popular in ancient China, with the dragon symbolizing the emperor and the phoenix the empress. They represented the harmony of husband and wife and also brought good luck. The phoenix was the feminine counterpart of the masculine dragon, representing the balance of yin and yang.

Twins were (and still are) considered a special blessing in Chinese families. A set of twins comprising a boy and a girl was especially auspicious, a sign of favor and fortune for the family. Even today, the Chinese refer to these boy and girl pairs as dragon-phoenix twins.

The phoenix's appearance in royal artifacts and architecture used by empresses highlighted its association with virtue and grace. In the Han dynasty, which began in 202 BCE, artists depicted a pair of phoenixes, male and female, on vases and other artwork. The male bird was "Fèng," and the female was "Huáng."

Fènghuáng, painted by Yu Sheng (1692–1767) [55]

According to Chinese mythology, after Pangu hatched from the cosmic egg at creation, Fènghuáng joined with the Dragon, Qilin, and Turtle to shape the cosmos. They created the five seasons (spring, summer, late Summer, autumn, and winter) and the five elements (earth, fire, metal, water, and wood). The phoenix ruled summer and fire, perceived as the giver of warmth and light.

The Four Benevolent Animals divided the world into five sections: east, west, north, south, and center. Fènghuáng, representing the south, controlled the five tones of traditional Chinese music, which are based on the pentatonic scale (gong, shang, jue, zhi, and yu). The phoenix sang to bring harmony to the heavens and held sovereignty over all the other birds. Fènghuáng symbolized the universe and the connection between Heaven and Earth. The bird's head was the sky, its eyes the sun, its back the moon, its feet the earth, and its tail the planets.

Fènghuáng was the herald of new dynasties. The Chinese believed that when the bird appeared, it was an omen of a new emperor coming to power who was not from the current ruling family. An emperor could lose the "Mandate of Heaven," the concept that Heaven gave the legitimacy to rule. The mandate depended more on the emperor's character than on his lineage. Only a virtuous, wise, and just ruler had Heaven's mandate.

The phoenix could not tolerate immorality. When evil reigned and vice took over, the phoenix disappeared. Fènghuáng refused to tolerate rulers who abused power or were deceitful. Such people would never see a phoenix. Floods and famines were signs that the current emperor had lost Heaven's mandate. If this happened, the Chinese could legitimately overthrow their emperor and install a new one. If people saw a Fènghuáng, it was a sign of blessing over the new dynasty.

A Fènghuáng would appear during the reign of benevolent rulers, confirming their legitimacy. When society lived in peace and harmony, the Fènghuáng was active in blessing the kingdom. When people saw the phoenix, it was a welcome sign that prosperity was coming their way. If they took note of where a Fènghuáng landed, a precious treasure was nearby. The Chinese phoenix was sheer goodness. It never sought revenge when wronged. It only blessed people, never cursing them. To avoid harming animals or even plants, the bird subsisted on morning dew.

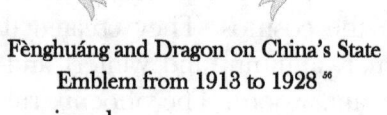

Fènghuáng and Dragon on China's State Emblem from 1913 to 1928 [46]

The Phoenix, the Dragon, and the Iridescent Pearl is a folktale about an adventure the pair had. Dragon enjoyed swimming in the cool river every day. Phoenix would accompany him but perch on a tree branch overlooking the river, as she did not want her feathers to get wet. One spring day, Dragon was enjoying a sunbath after his swim.

"Fènghuáng, if we followed this river downstream, where would it take us?"

Phoenix had traveled extensively, acquiring wisdom and knowledge. "Lóng (Dragon), my dear, it flows to the sea, as most rivers do," she replied.

"I have never seen the sea," Lóng remarked. "Fènghuáng, let's go on an adventure! We'll fly to the sea."

So Fènghuáng and Lóng flew into the air and traveled all day. They finally reached the seashore just in time to watch a glorious sky painted in pink, purple, and red as the sun sank under the waves.

"How beautiful! What an exciting day!" Lóng exclaimed. "Fènghuáng, I want to see more. Tomorrow, let's fly over the sea!"

The next day, the couple flew across the sea until they arrived at an island with palm trees and gleaming white sand.

"Wa!" Lóng exclaimed. "Such pure beauty! Look at these waterfalls and those lovely flowers. I have never seen anything like this!"

Fènghuáng agreed. "This truly is an exquisite place!"

The pair rested by a lake where the waterfall emptied. "Lóng! Look at that pebble on the lake bottom. It appears to be glowing."

Lóng peered down. "Maybe it's just the sun reflecting off it. Still, I'll dive in and grab it."

Minutes later, Lóng was back. "Look, Fènghuáng! It really is shining."

"Ah," Fènghuáng breathed. "This must be a precious stone!"

Below them, they heard a surly voice rising from the water. "Yes! It is quite precious. You are holding a magic pearl."

The two looked down to see a crab waving its enormous claws. "You must put it back immediately! The pearl's magic is why this island is extraordinary!"

"In that case, Fènghuáng, I think we must become the guardians of this pearl. We must preserve this enchanted island," Lóng said.

And so, the couple settled down on the lovely island. However, trouble was brewing in a distant land.

Luxuries surrounded a spoiled and self-indulgent princess, yet she always wanted more. She heard of the resplendent pearl on the magnificent island.

"I must have it for myself. Bǎobiāo!" she called her personal guard. "Go to that island and steal that pearl!"

The guard sneaked onto the island and stole the pearl when Lóng and Fènghuáng were enjoying their noontime nap. He traveled back to the distant realm and presented the priceless pearl to the princess.

"Ah! This must be the world's most glorious jewel. Look how it glows! My brilliant treasure, now you're mine!" she said.

But then, the princess frowned. "This glowing pearl is so bright, it's lighting up the sky. People will discover the cause of the radiance and find out that I stole it. We have to hide it away. Bǎobiāo! Take me to the mountain fortress!"

The princess hid the pearl away in an underground vault in the fortress. Yet, a few months later, she threw a birthday party for herself at the fortress. She could not resist bringing out the pearl to show her guests. The dazzling pearl was so bright that it was difficult to look at it directly. It glowed even more than when the princess first stole it, so brilliantly that it lit up the sky like the sun. It caught the attention of Lóng and Fènghuáng, who had been flying from one place to another, looking for the radiant pearl.

Fènghuáng flew at the speed of light toward the mountain fortress, swept through a window, and snatched up the pearl from the princess's hand with her claws. Flapping her wings, Fènghuáng flew out the window, but she had trouble holding on to the pearl. Suddenly, it slipped from her claw and dropped to the mountain. Fènghuáng dived after the pearl as it rolled down the slope. Suddenly, she heard a crash of thunder and saw a blinding light.

For a moment, Fènghuáng could see nothing. Then, she caught sight of the glowing pearl.

"Āiyā!" she exclaimed. "The pearl is melting!"

Just at that moment, Lóng caught up with her. "Look, Fènghuáng! The pearl is dissolving into water! See that spectacular emerald-green lake covering everything?"

Then, Lóng frowned. "Fènghuáng, I failed to protect the pearl when it was on the island. Now, it is my duty to guard the lake. I will never leave it! I will stand over it forever!"

In an instant, Lóng turned himself into a majestic mountain rising from the lakeshore.

"I will never leave you, my love!" said Fènghuáng. "I also must atone for letting the pearl be stolen." She transformed into a mountain guarding the lake's opposite shore. The emerald lake still glistens in China, with two high mountains standing guard on its shores.

Hui and the Golden Pheasant is a folktale about a peasant and a pheasant. The peasant, Hui, swindled a well-meaning man, but in the end, the man who was swindled was rewarded.

Hui was a farmer who struggled to make ends meet, yet he had grandiose dreams. He had raised a magnificent golden pheasant and decided to sell it in the city. He knew he would get a reasonable price for such a beautiful bird.

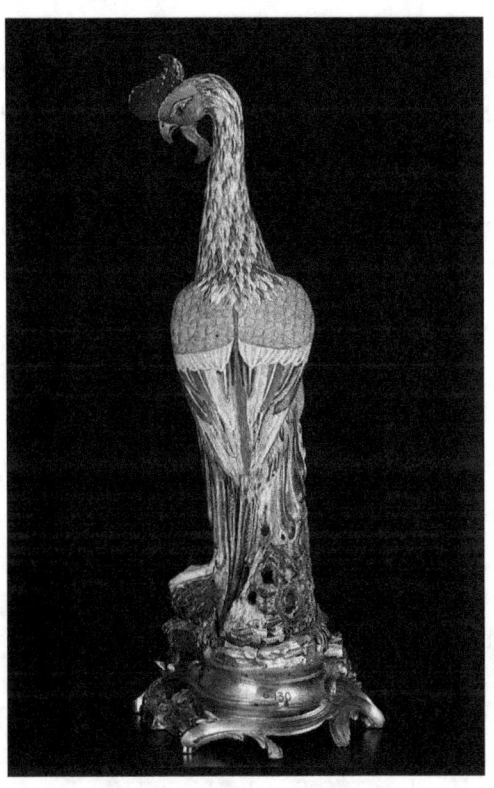

Qing dynasty porcelain Fènghuáng"

As he walked down the road carrying his pheasant in a cage, Hui daydreamed of what he would do with the money from selling the pheasant. "Maybe I could start my own business. Yes! I'll get rich and build a marvelous mansion. Then, a beautiful lady of means will fall in love with me, and we will get married. That's not all! I'll invent something ingenious. It will change people's lives and make me famous. I'll travel the world."

Hui's thoughts turned to Fènghuáng. "The bird always appears as a herald of favorable fortune and blessing. You, my lovely pheasant, are my Fènghuáng! You will bring me a wonderful future!"

Hui's fanciful fantasies were cut short when someone cleared their throat. It was a man named Enlai who had a curious nature.

"Excuse me," Enlai said. "I couldn't help but notice your broad smile. What is making you so happy?"

"Oh! My Fènghuáng is making me happy!"

"Your Fènghuáng?" Enlai questioned, puzzled. He stared at the bird in the cage. Wasn't it a golden pheasant? It had a bright golden head and back, a scarlet breast, and purple and blue on its wings and tail. He cocked his head in bewilderment. "Is this bird a Fènghuáng?"

"Oh, yes!" Hui smiled broadly. "This is my Fènghuáng. He will bring me immeasurable wealth and good fortune."

Enlai thought to himself, "If I buy this bird, I could give it as a gift to the king of Chu. He will consider it a sign of the Mandate of Heaven! Then, he will give me a substantial reward. I'll be rich and powerful!"

"May I buy your bird?" asked Enlai.

"Yes, but only at a high price."

Enlai was wealthy and considered the purchase an investment. "How about a thousand silver pieces?"

Hui cocked his head. "Make it two thousand, and it is yours!"

Enlai happily agreed and handed over two thousand silver coins. Hui handed him the cage with the pheasant.

Enlai excitedly traveled toward the capital of Chu, eager to take his expensive and invaluable gift to the king. It was a journey of several days, and he told everyone he met about the mythical bird he carried, which was to be a gift for the king. Word traveled fast, and soon the king heard about the gift coming his way.

Unfortunately, Enlai had forgotten to ask Hui how to care for the bird. He knew nothing about giving the bird water or what it liked to eat. After two days on the road, he spent the night at an inn and was horrified to find the bird dead the next morning.

"Oh! This is terrible! I did not know a Fènghuáng could die! Aren't they supposed to be immortal? Now, I have no gift for the king. I certainly will never see a Fènghuáng again!"

Several days later, Enlai received a message that the king wanted him to come to his palace. Enlai was confused, but he went anyway.

"Sir," he said to the king when he arrived. "I had hoped to bring you a fantastic gift. Sadly, now I cannot."

"I know," answered the king. "Word reached me that you were bringing me a Fènghuáng."

"I was, but he died."

"Yes, I heard. I did not know a Fènghuáng could die."

"Nor did I," sighed Enlai.

"Nevertheless, I am deeply touched by your intentions. Your thoughtfulness and largesse are beyond compare. Just knowing that you would bring me such an astounding gift is a blessing. For that, I will reward you!"

The king gave Enlai a position in his court and forty thousand silver pieces, twenty times what Enlai had paid Hui. The so-called Fènghuáng turned out to be auspicious for both Hui and Enlai.

Chapter 8: Warriors of Destiny

This chapter highlights the epic tales of legendary Chinese warriors with fates inextricably linked to the destinies of empires and realms. These heroes were famous for their unparalleled military expertise, exceptional bravery, brilliant strategies, and astounding combat skills.

These warriors had a destiny. In Chinese culture, the concept of destiny often signifies a preordained path that heroes are meant to fulfill, marked by trials and exceptional deeds. Destiny (mìngyùn) includes one's absolute, predetermined fate (mìng) plus elements based on one's choices, cosmic forces, and luck (yùn). Destiny is not entirely fixed; it has some flexibility. A person's actions and choices influence their lives.

Guan Yu

One of China's best-known warriors of destiny was Guan Yu (160–220 CE), a general at the end of the Han dynasty. Guan Yu possessed stellar military prowess, wielding a weapon called the "Green Dragon Crescent Blade." His weapon was a "guandao," a heavy, notched blade on a pole about five feet long. Guan Yu's history appears in the *Records of the Three Kingdoms*, written in the Sui dynasty (581–618 CE). By this point, people worshiped Guan Yu as a god. He was a dominant character in Luo Guanzhong's novel, *Romance of the Three Kingdoms,* written in the Yuan dynasty (1279–1368 CE).

When Guan Yu was in his early twenties, the Yellow Turban Rebellion, a peasant revolt, broke out. Near Guan Yu's hometown, a man named Liu Bei was reading a notice of the rebellion posted on a wall. He was a descendant of the fourth emperor of the Han dynasty, but his family had fallen into poverty after his father's death. Liu Bei was weaving straw sandals and grass mats to support his family. He sighed at the news of the revolt.

"Sir!" spoke a raspy voice behind him. "Why don't you help your country?"

Liu Bei swirled around to see a dark-skinned man with unruly hair. "Who are you?"

"My name is Zhang Fei. I have a farm near here, and I sell wine and meat."

Liu Bei introduced himself. "I'm a member of the imperial family, but we have fallen on hard times. I would love to fight for my country, but I have no money for armor or weapons."

"Well, I have the means to outfit a militia," Zhang Fei replied. "Why don't you and I raise some troops and defend our land?"

The two young men set off to the village inn to discuss their plans. Shortly after, Guan Yu walked into the inn and ordered wine. He was close to seven feet tall, with an eighteen-inch beard, a dark red face, and eyebrows that looked like silkworms.

"Bring it quickly!" ordered Guan Yu. "I'm on my way to join the army."

Liu Bei looked over his massive frame, then picked up his drink and sat down next to Guan Yu. "I'm Liu Bei. What is your name?"

"My name is Guan Yu. I used to live on the other side of the river, but I've been on the run for five years."

"Why?" asked Liu Bei.

"When I was a teenager, I killed a man. He deserved it. He was a thug and a bully who was hurting people. But he was also rich and powerful, so I had to leave town."

Liu Bei smiled. "My friend and I are putting together a militia to defend our country. Would you like to join us?"

Guan Yu nodded eagerly, and the three men walked off together to Zhang Fei's farm. "Let's go to the peach orchard behind my house," Zhang Fei said. "The flowers are in bloom. We should offer a sacrifice, asking for Heaven's blessing and swearing our intentions to fight together."

The *Romance of the Three Kingdoms* tells the story of the "Peach Garden Oath." Liu Bei held a ceremony in the peach orchard, where they sacrificed a white horse, a black ox, and wine. Liu Bei named Guan Yu as his younger brother and Zhang Fei as his youngest brother. The three men kneeled together and swore this oath:

> "Though we have different names, we are brothers. We swear to cooperate with each other, rescue each other, assist each other in times of distress and danger, honor our nation, and protect the people. May Heaven permit the three of us to die on the same day. May the gods confirm what is in our hearts, yet if we betray the brotherhood, or turn away from kindness and righteousness, may Heaven strike us down."

Guan Yu and Zhang Fei stood up and bowed before Liu Bei, offering him fraternal piety as their older brother. They then invited the local villagers to a feast, where they ate the ox and horse. Three hundred men came, and they recruited them for their militia. Some wealthy merchants helped outfit the new militia with horses, weapons, and armor. The three "brothers" fought together and were fiercely loyal to each other in the long struggle to reunite China. They slept in the same room and ate from the same pot.

However, they failed to preserve the Han dynasty. The uprising and other factors led to the Han dynasty's fall. A fragmented China entered the Three Kingdoms period (220–280 CE), during which warlords ruled three states. Liu Bei became the warlord over the state of Shu Han (primarily today's Guizhou, Sichuan, and Yunnan provinces in southwest China). He considered his state the legitimate continuation of the Han dynasty. Guan Yu and Zhang Fei became his generals and bodyguards.

Guan Yu was revered not only for his martial prowess, immortalized in folklore, but also for his loyalty, sense of honor, and strict code of behavior. His loyalty to Liu Bei was put to the test when Cao Cao, warlord of the Cao Wei kingdom in north China, captured him. Cao Cao and Liu Bei were archrivals, but Cao Cao had heard of Guan Yu's incomparable fighting skills. Instead of executing Guan Yu, he gave him gifts and offered him a position as an officer in his military.

Having no real choice, Guan Yu took the pragmatic route and served his new lord for a time. However, after killing Cao Cao's two arch enemies, Guan Yu politely refused Cao Cao's gifts.

"Sir, the best gift you can give me is my freedom," he said. "Let me return to my brother, Liu Bei. We have made an oath to fight together and die together."

Cao Cao released Guan Yu, who hurried back just in time to rescue Liu Bei from desperate straits. Years later, Guan Yu repaid Cao Cao for giving him his freedom. Cao Cao was fleeing a battle that had turned into a disaster for him. Instead of chasing him down, Guan Yu let Cao Cao escape.

Sun Quan was the warlord of the Wu kingdom in eastern China. While Lu Bei and Cao Cao fought each other fiercely, Sun Quan mostly stayed out of the fray. At one point, he allied with Lu Bei to successfully fight Cao Cao. Lu Bei and Sun Quan formed an uneasy alliance, and Sun Quan defeated Cao Cao.

However, Sun Quan criticized Guan Yu for stealing his food supply and constantly stirring up hostilities. His army succeeded in capturing Guan Yu. Sun Quan originally planned to keep Guan Yu alive to fight with him against Lu Bei.

But his advisors warned him against this plan. "A wolf shouldn't be kept as a pet as it'll bring harm to the keeper," they said. "Guan Yu and Lu Bei are sworn brothers. He will never agree to fight Lu Bei."

Thus, Sun Quan executed Guan Yu and sent his head to Cao Cao, who gave him a proper hero's burial.

Guan Yu, top, holds the Green Dragon. Lu Bei is on the left and Zhang on the right. Silk painting by Japanese artist, Sekkan Sakurai (1715-1790). [58]

Hua Mulan

Hua Mulan, made famous by the 1998 Disney movie, was a legendary female warrior who disguised herself as a man to take her father's place in the army. Her story challenges traditional gender roles and exemplifies themes of duty and honor. Mulan's name means "magnolia," and the *Ballad of Mulan,* written in the Northern Wei dynasty (386–534 CE) is the source for her ancient tale. The ballad contains only 392 Chinese characters. In Chinese writing, each character usually represents a word, but some only represent sounds; thus, Mulan's tale is a short story.

Nevertheless, it powerfully serves to remind folks that China has heroines. Mulan's ballad of devotion and loyalty to her family centers on the Chinese values of filial piety and patriotism. She was devoted to her parents and her country yet also brave and selfless when facing adversity. Her story reminds us that all have the strength to fulfill their destinies; however, we must cultivate our spirits so we have reserves of courage. Here is Mulan's story.

Mulan sat weaving near the door of her home, sighing. What was she thinking about that made her so gloomy? Was there a boy in her heart?

"No," answered Mulan. "I am not thinking about a boy. There is no boy in my heart. I am melancholy for another reason. Last night, I saw the list of draftees that our emperor has picked to fight for him. My father's name is on the list, yet, he is too old and sick to fight! He has no grown son who can fight in his place. There is only one thing to do. I will buy a horse and go fight in my father's place!"

Mulan headed east and bought a fine warhorse; then she bought a bridle in the south. In the west, she purchased a saddle blanket; in the north, she bought a long whip. Once outfitted, she bid her parents farewell at dawn. She rode all day and arrived at the Yellow River at dusk. She camped that evening next to the river. At sunset, it seemed eerily quiet. All she could hear was the water gently splashing the rocks and the melodious call of the Huà Méi thrush. She was used to her bustling village and the familiar sounds of people calling out to each other in the evening.

At dawn, she left the Yellow River and rode toward the soaring Black Mountains. That night, she camped out again, missing the sounds of her parents calling her. Now, all she heard was the roar of Heishan bandits far away. Mulan continued riding to war for ten thousand miles, flying through mountain passes, with her iron armor gleaming in the sunlight. Finally, she heard the sentry's gong. She had arrived at the battle.

A hundred battles were fought over the next twelve years. Generals and heroes died, rising to meet the Jade Emperor on high, enthroned in the Hall of Brilliance. The Son of Heaven held twelve scrolls listing their merits and gave thousands of rewards. As the war ended, the emperor passed out earthly rewards to the heroes who had survived.

"What do you desire?" the emperor asked Mulan.

"I have no need of a lord's title," she answered. "Just give me a swift horse so I can ride home."

When Mulan's parents heard she had returned, they rushed out to welcome her home. Her younger brother roasted a pig and a sheep to celebrate her return. Mulan rode up with her comrades-in-arms, then left them to go into her room.

"I just want to sit in my chair, take off my war cloak, and put on my old clothes—girl's clothing!" she whispered to herself.

Mulan combed her hair, wove yellow flowers into her braids, and put on makeup. Then, she walked outside into the courtyard to join the men with whom she had fought for twelve years. All that time they thought she was a man.

"Mulan!" the soldiers cried. "We never realized you were a lady!"

Mulan's story led to the saying, "When two deer run together, one can tell the buck from the doe. But when two rabbits run together, how does one know which is the male and which is the female?"

Hua Mulan's return. Mural at Dalongdong Baoan Temple in Taiwan by Pan Li-shui[19]

Yue Fei

The life journey of Yue Fei (1103-1142 CE) is a symbol of loyalty and patriotism in Chinese culture. His outstanding military campaigns and the tragic turn of events leading to his wrongful execution turned him into a martyr in the eyes of the people. General Yue Fei was renowned for his excellence on the battlefield and his exemplary ethics, especially his patriotism and trustworthiness.

This celebrated general was born in the Northern Song dynasty; however, when he was in his early twenties, Jurchen warriors from northeast China and Russia invaded. They captured the emperor and hundreds of his officials. This forced the Song dynasty, led by the emperor's younger brother, to move south of the Yangtze River, after which it was called the Southern Song.

In his late teens, Yue Fei received military training. People whispered, "Have you seen what he can do? He's superhuman! He can shoot a bow with both his right and left hands! And that's not all. He can draw a bow of four hundred pounds! His spear fighting is unparalleled."

At the time the Jurchens invaded, a dilemma confronted Yue Fei. His father had recently died. He desperately wanted to defend his country from the fierce marauders, yet his absence would leave no one to provide for his mother. He was torn between filial piety and patriotism.

"Yue Fei, take off your shirt," his mother commanded. When Yue Fei bared his back, his mother tattooed four characters: "Jīng zhōng bào guó," or "Serve the country with loyalty."

With his mother's blessing, Yue Fei rode off to fight the Jurchens. He never lost a battle. He once led a small band of 500 men to victory over 100,000 Jurchen soldiers. Yue Fei not only kept the Jurchen at bay but also prevented rival Chinese factions from destroying the Southern Song dynasty.

In addition to his courage and uncanny tactics, Yue Fei was a man of honor. He protected the common people by strictly forbidding his soldiers from looting their farms and villages when passing through. Yet, he also ensured his soldiers had the supplies they needed. He tended them when they were sick. When his soldiers died in battle, he took care of their families. When the emperor rewarded him, he shared the bounty with his men.

Once, Yue Fei squelched a rebellion of citizens unwilling to recognize their new emperor. However, he hesitated when the emperor commanded, "Execute everyone in the city! We have to set an example!"

"Sir!" Yue Fei pleaded. "Surely, we should not kill everyone. Please command me to execute the ringleaders of the rebellion, but spare the ordinary people. Then, they will be thankful for your mercy and loyal to you forever."

The emperor agreed to Yue Fei's suggestion. "Yue Fei, you are shrewd! I appreciate your loyalty to me and your care for the people's welfare."

Yet, Yue Fei had enemies. His popularity with the emperor and his soldiers made them jealous. They whispered to the emperor, "Yue Fei is a long way from your capital. He's getting too powerful. The local people are devoted to him. What's keeping him from instigating his own rebellion against you?"

The emperor recalled Yue Fei, who was at the cusp of retaking Kaifeng from the Jurchens. Kaifeng was China's largest and most prosperous city at the time. Yue Fei obediently returned but remarked, "I spent ten years securing this territory from the Jurchen invaders. When I leave, they'll grab it back in a flash."

When Yue Fei arrived at the capital, his enemies at court convinced the emperor to revoke his position as general. Months later, they presented trumped-up charges, and Yue Fei, still in his thirties, was sentenced to die. Legend says that after his death, black mist swirled through the sky.

Statue of Yue Fei at his tomb and shrine in Hangzhou [60]

Chapter 9: Mountains and Rivers: Magical Landscapes

Natural landscapes hold a prominent role in Chinese folklore. Mountains and rivers are not just physical features; they are imbued with spiritual significance and magical qualities. In the Chinese worldview, the natural world impacts human life. Mountains are the home of gods, spirits, and sages. Medicinal plants grow on mountains, and pilgrims travel to mountains to meditate and seek enlightenment. Since mountains are sacred, most mountains in China have small shrines, and many have temples and monasteries.

Rivers bring life, change, and nourishment. Chinese civilization emerged in the fertile regions along the Yellow and Yangtze rivers, foundational pillars of Chinese culture. The Chinese called the Yellow River their "Mother River" but also "China's Sorrow." Rivers enable transportation and irrigation for farming, but they are also agents of chaos when they flood. In Chinese folklore, rivers are home to water spirits and sometimes even dragons.

Mount Tai, in eastern China's Shandong Province, stands five thousand feet high and is one of China's Five Sacred Mountains. The ancient Chinese considered it a holy place where emperors would perform rituals to ensure the country's prosperity and peace. In Chinese legends, it served as a meeting point between the divine and the earthly. As the eastern-most mountain of the Five Sacred Mountains, Mount Tai represented birth, renewal, and the sunrise.

Chinese emperors traveled to Mount Tai to offer the Feng Shan sacrifices of food and jade items. At the foot of the mountain, the emperor honored Earth, and at the mountaintop, he honored Heaven. The sacrifices enabled the emperor to receive the Mandate of Heaven. Even Japan, Korea, and states in Central Asia sent representatives to attend the Feng Shan sacrifices in the Tang dynasty.

The "Great Deity of Mount Tai" was the **Dongyue Emperor**, the mountain's supreme god. He was also the god of the underworld, deciding how long each human should live. His wife (or daughter) was Bixia Yuanjun, the "Goddess of the Blue Dawn" or the "Heavenly Jade Lady." She was the deity of destiny and childbirth.

The Dongyue Emperor was not always a god. At one time, he was Prince Wucheng of the Shang dynasty (1600-1046 BCE) serving in King Zhou's court. King Zhou was infatuated with his concubine named Daji. He failed to realize Daji was not really a woman but a fox spirit (húlí jīng). Fox spirits, or vixen spirits, could shapeshift. They had nine tails; eight extended from the main tail. Some fox spirits were benevolent spirits, and others were evil. Daji was an evil húlí jīng.

A vixen spirit from a Chinese tomb mural, late fourth to mid-fifth century CE.[61]

King Zhou always had abysmal character, but after consorting with Daji, he worsened. He cruelly tortured his ministers who dared suggest a different opinion. The king became enamored with Prince Wucheng's wife, Lady Jia, and tried to violate her. She committed suicide rather than submit to his advances. Wucheng's sister Huang was another concubine of the despicable king. When she heard what happened to Lady Jia, she scolded King Zhou, and he angrily threw her from his tower window to her death.

After his wife and sister died at King Zhou's hands, Prince Wucheng defected to the rival state of Zhou, where King Wu was trying to topple the Shang dynasty. Wu eventually won the war and established the new Zhou dynasty. However, Prince Wucheng died in the Battle of Muye, which brought the ultimate victory. For avenging unrighteousness, Heaven appointed him as the Dongyue Emperor, supreme leader over the gods of the Five Sacred Mountains.

The **Legend of the White Snake** is one of China's most endearing love stories. It centers on a young man named Xu Xian and a white snake spirit named Bai Suzhen (Lady Bai). Lady Bai was once a malevolent demon, but she reformed and spent one thousand years studying the principles of Tao on Mount Emei. The Dragon King of the East China Sea changed her into a woman, although she could still shapeshift into a snake.

Lady Bai's next goal was to earn immortality through good deeds, and she became a disciple of Lishan Laomu, the Tao goddess of Mount Li. One day, Lady Bai saw a beggar hitting a green snake with a club and intervened, saving the snake. The green snake promised to stay with Lady Bai forever, so she nicknamed the snake Qingmei, meaning "green sister."

Later, Lady Bai traveled to West Lake in Hangzhou. On Tomb Sweeping Day, she met a man named Xu Xian at the Broken Bridge. She recognized him from a past life—he had rescued her from a deadly danger. Xu Xian and Lady Bai fell in love, married, and had a baby boy. Yet, trouble soon erupted. A Buddhist monk named Fahai recognized Lady Bai's true identity.

"Your wife is not a true human. She's a snake spirit!"

"You're insane! My wife isn't a snake; she's a woman!" Xu Xian protested.

"If you don't believe me, test it out," Fahai said. "Dragon Boat Festival is coming up. Have her drink realgar wine. See what happens."

(Realgar is an arsenic sulfide mineral that the Chinese traditionally mixed into their wine at the Dragon Boat Festival. They believed it drove away evil spirits, illnesses, and insects.)

Xu Xian gave Lady Bai some realgar wine at the Dragon Boat Festival, and she suddenly morphed into a large white snake.

"Ahhhh!" screamed Xu Xian. He had a heart attack and died on the spot.

"Oh, my darling! You can't die!" Lady Bai cried. She flew to Mount Emei, where a special fungus called lingzhi grew. She hurried back to her husband and used the immortal fungus to revive him.

"Lady Bai, I still love you, even if you are a snake," gasped Xu Xian. Lady Bai embraced and kissed him, but she knew the danger was not over. The monk Fahai was still out there.

She was right. Fahai came after Lady Bai, captured her, and locked her in the Leifeng Pagoda in Hangzhou. Xu Xian searched all over China for his wife. When he heard she was imprisoned at the Leifeng Pagoda, he traveled there and tried to free her, but Fahai's sorcery was too strong. Xu Xian became a monk at the nearby monastery so he could stay close to his wife. He gave baby Xu Shilin to Qingmei, his wife's green snake friend. Xu Shilin grew up to be a scholar and finally rescued his mother from the Leifeng Pagoda.

A wood carving of Lady Bai at the Leifeng Pagoda on Sunset Mountain[68]

Another Chinese folktale about a mountain is **Emperor Qin Shi Huang's Search for Mount Penglai.** Qin Shi Huang was the first emperor of the Qin dynasty (221-206 BCE), and he was obsessed with immortality.

"How can I live forever? What must I do?" he persistently asked.

One of his ministers rubbed his beard. "I have heard stories about Mount Penglai. It is a white spirit mountain in the center of the sea where eight immortals live in a splendid palace. Legend says that the fruit growing on the magical island trees can heal all diseases, make a person forever young, and even revive the dead."

The emperor leaned forward with excitement. "Xu Fu!" he called to his court sorcerer. "Take ten exquisite ships and five hundred children. Choose the handsomest boys and the most beautiful girls. Sail across the Eastern Sea until you find the magical white mountain, then bring me the fruit of immortality."

Why did Emperor Qin send five hundred children? Perhaps they were to colonize the heavenly island. Sorcerer Xu Fu found a large island with a high, snow-covered mountain. (It might have been Mount Fuji on Japan's Honshu Island.) However, he could not find the fruit of immortality, so he sailed back to China. Later, he sailed east again but never returned. Emperor Qin fell into despair, searching desperately for another way to live forever.

A painting of one of the ships sent to find the Island of Immortality [68]

Rivers, home to water spirits and the occasional dragon, featured in many Chinese folktales. One was the story of **Lady Meng Jiang**. Meng Jiang and her husband, Qi Liang, were newlyweds and hoping to start a family. However, the emperor had started a project to renovate and add on to the Great Wall of China. Since the wall was over 13,000 miles long, the emperor needed a million men to do the work. Meng Jiang's husband was among the many the emperor drafted to labor on the wall.

Meng Jiang stayed at home, worrying about Qi Liang. After many months, some men in their town returned from their duty on the wall, but her husband was not among them. She was horrified when she heard about the conditions the men worked under.

"We were lucky to survive," the men told her. "Never enough food. Many men died of starvation or were worked to death. The wall is mostly in the mountains, and it is cold for much of the year. Then, the landslides swept some workers away. Leopards and bears preyed on us."

Meng Jiang fretted. "My poor husband, working so hard with little food."

That night, she had a nightmare in which she saw her husband at the wall. "Meng Jiang!" he cried. "I'm so cold!"

Meng Jiang awakened and determined to travel to her husband. "Winter is coming soon. I must go to Qi Liang! I'll take warm clothing and food."

She traveled to the wall, but when she got there, she had difficulty finding the section on which her husband was working. Finally, she met some other men from her region.

"Brothers!" she cried. "Where is my husband?"

They looked at her sadly. "Little sister, Qi Liang died."

"No!" wailed Meng Jiang. "Where is he buried?"

"Oh, little sister, we don't even know. You see, the wall is actually two parallel walls, built of stone or brick. We fill in the middle with rubble, rocks, and packed earth. When one of us dies, we just lay him in that middle section and cover him with rubble and dirt. Countless men are buried within the wall's structure. We are so sorry."

Meng Jiang flung herself to the ground next to the wall, weeping. Her piercing wails were so loud that the earth shook, and a section of the wall crumbled. The construction workers fled, snatching up Meng Jiang and escaping the falling bricks and stones. When the dust settled, Meng Jiang peered at the wall.

"Look! Among that rubble! See those bones? Could they be my husband's?"

"Maybe," the men said. "That is the area where we buried Qi Liang. But we buried several other men with him."

"I'll prick my finger and let the blood drip on the bones. My blood will only penetrate my husband's bones!"

Thus, Lady Meng Jiang identified her husband's remains and gave him a proper burial with the usual rites. Meanwhile, the emperor, who had been inspecting work on the Great Wall, reached the section where Qi Liang died. He heard about how Lady Meng Jiang's wails caused the wall to collapse, exposing her husband's bones.

"What a story!" remarked the emperor. "I must meet this woman!"

When they brought Lady Meng Jiang to meet him, he was awestruck by her beauty.

"Marry me, Lady Meng!"

"But you already have several wives and dozens of concubines."

"I know, but none of them has your strength of character."

"Well," Meng Jiang answered. "I'll marry you if you do three things."

"Anything! Just name them!"

"First, you must order a forty-nine-day festival to honor my husband. I must properly mourn him before I can marry again. Second, you and all your officials must attend the festival. You need to honor all the thousands of men who have died working on your project. Third, you must build a forty-nine-foot-high terrace over the river. I will stand on it to offer a sacrifice to my husband."

"Yes! Yes! I'll do all three things," the emperor eagerly answered.

At the end of the forty-nine-day festival, Lady Meng Jiang climbed to the top of the platform over the river. She turned to the emperor. "My sacrifice is myself! I'm going to join my husband!"

At that, Meng Jiang leaped into the river and drowned.

A section of the Great Wall in the mountains[64]

The **Xiang River Goddesses** were once princesses, the daughters of the legendary Emperor Yao. Their names were E Huang (Fairy Radiance) and Nu Ying (Maiden Bloom). Emperor Yao ruled over the Yellow River Valley in northeastern China during the 2200s BCE. "History" from this era is more likely to be folktales, as China did not develop writing for another thousand years. Yao was the emperor at the beginning of China's Great Flood.

In those days, China's rulers were not hereditary. The king chose a leader to succeed him based on merit, not kinship. Emperor Yao chose one of his ministers, Shun, to inherit his throne. He handed the throne over to Shun years before he died because he had failed to control the devastating, years-long flooding. By this time, Emperor Yao had given his daughters E Huang and Nu Ying in marriage to Shun.

The young ladies loved their husband and had a good relationship with each other. When they were newly married and Shun was not yet king, the sisters heard that Shun's evil father, stepmother, and half-brother were plotting to murder him. The morally bankrupt trio wanted to steal the dowry of sheep, cattle, and grain that Emperor Yao had given Shun. E Huang and Nu Ying warned their new husband and gave him a magical bird coat for protection. Shun's father told him to go up on the barn to mend the roof. Once he was up there, they set the barn on fire and took the ladder away. However, wearing his magical bird coat, Shun flew safely to the ground.

Shun's despicable relatives then threw him into a well to drown. However, the sisters had anticipated this and given him a magic dragon coat. He swam underwater through a conduit leading to the well and escaped. Next, the sisters bathed their husband in a magic antidote, which thwarted another murder attempt by his homicidal family. Finally, Emperor Yao removed Shun and his wives from the bloodthirsty family and brought them to court.

Shun eventually became the emperor, and all went well. He offered sacrifices to Shang Di, the Supreme God, then offered burnt offerings at China's sacred mountains. He also offered sacrifices to the Yellow River and Yangtze River. Yu the Engineer stopped the flooding that was devastating the realm, and Shun appointed him as his successor.

E Huang and Nu Ying [65]

Then, after Shun was emperor for fifty years, disaster struck. He was on a military expedition against the Miao near the headwaters of the Xiang River. He missed his footing, fell into the water, and the raging current swept him away, never to be seen again. His two wives rushed to the region, desperately searching for their husband, to no avail. As E Huang and Nu Ying sat by the river weeping, their tears stained the bamboo shoots. To this day, the bamboo in that area has spots. Finally, the two sisters flung themselves into the river to join their husband in death. They reincarnated as the Xiang River goddesses, the subject of Chinese poetry for millennia.

Chapter 10: Magical Lanterns and Chinese Festivals

Chinese folklore often explains the reason behind Chinese festivals. Other times, the stories take place during a key festival. China's Lantern Festival marks the end of the two-week Chinese New Year celebration. Red lanterns adorn the streets, symbolizing auspicious fortune and driving away malevolent spirits. This chapter unravels the mythology behind the lanterns. Another key celebration featuring lanterns is the Mid-Autumn Festival, and we'll explore how and why it is observed.

A Qing dynasty rank badge with a crane motif [66]

One popular folktale that explains the origin of the Lantern Festival is the **Legend of the Jade Emperor's Crane**. In this story, the Jade Emperor had a favorite celestial crane that adorned his heavenly palace garden. One day, the crane flew from Heaven down to Earth, where he foraged for germinating seeds and sprouted plants next to a village. Not realizing he was the Jade Emperor's crane, the villagers killed him because he was harming their crops.

When the Jade Emperor found out what had happened to his crane, his anger erupted. "I shall send a massive fire to destroy this village on the fifteenth day of the first lunar month!"

However, one of the Jade Emperor's seven daughters flew down to Earth to warn the villagers of the impending inferno.

"What can we do?" the villagers wondered. "How can we avoid the fire?"

They visited Shèngrén, a wise old man who lived in a nearby village.

Shèngrén threw some dàmá leaves on a brazier and pondered the perplexing problem as he breathed in the smoke. His brow furrowed as the villagers looked on anxiously. Finally, he brightened.

"Trick the Jade Emperor!" he advised. "Make him think your village is already going up in smoke."

"How?" asked the villagers.

"For three days, burn enormous bonfires in the streets. Don't forget to set off firecrackers and light red lanterns. Do this on the fifteenth day of the first lunar month and for two days prior."

The villagers followed Shèngrén's advice. When the Jade Emperor's celestial soldiers arrived to immolate the village, they saw billowing black smoke and flames leaping up from various points of the village. They heard explosions, and the entire village glowed red from the burning lanterns.

"Someone has done our work for us!" the troops laughed as they gazed at the spectacular display. "An enemy tribe must have attacked them."

They flew back to Heaven and reported to the Jade Emperor that the village was already destroyed. Back on Earth, the villagers breathed a sigh of relief. Each year, they celebrated their narrow escape by lighting red lanterns, setting off fireworks, and burning bonfires. Some brave souls even leaped over the fires. The village's annual tradition spread throughout the land until all of China celebrated it.

Chinese red lanterns [97]

Another tale about the Chinese red lanterns, **Laozu and the Nian Monster**, casts the Jade Emperor in a more benevolent, protective light. He passed a heavenly decree for the people to use red lanterns to protect themselves from a mythical beast called a nian. This creature lived inside mountains or under the sea. However, its name is the same as the Chinese word for "year." The ancient Chinese believed it came out of the sea or mountains at the new year. The Chinese phrase "guònián" means "pass (celebrate) the new year," but it can also carry the meaning of getting the nian monster to pass or leave.

At New Year (in January or February, depending on the Chinese lunar calendar), the nian was ravenous and ready to eat. In the dead of winter, food was hard to find in the wild, so it would come into villages or towns. It raided food stores, ate the village dogs and chickens, and even ate people, especially children. The nian's head looked like a lion with a flat face and long fangs. Its body was more like a dog.

The beast disliked fire, the color red, and loud noise, so people banged drums, set off firecrackers, lit bonfires, wore red clothing, and hung red banners and red lanterns everywhere. They left food outside the house for the beast so it would not eat people. At the Chinese New Year, two men put on a lion costume and performed the lion dance to the sound of drums and gongs. The lion dance chased away evil spirits and the nian monster. It brought luck and prosperity to the new year.

A Taoist monk named Hongjun Laozu tricked the nian monster. He climbed up the mountain where the nian lived and found it in a cave.

"Nian," he said, "I am a peaceful monk. I mean you no harm. But I want you to stop eating people. Stop frightening them. Let them enjoy celebrating the New Year."

The nian laughed. "Haha! You've come into my lair. Thank you for delivering my food today. I'll enjoy eating you."

"Oh, but I'm just an old man," remarked Hongjun. "I'm not delicious. Tell me, do you eat the poisonous snakes living on this mountain?"

"Of course!" sneered the tian. "Let me show you."

The monster left the cave, gathered up some snakes, and ate them. When it got back to the cave, Hongjun asked, "What about those wild beasts lurking on the back of the mountain? Are you powerful enough to tame them?"

"Certainly!" replied the nian. It left for a while, then returned. "The wild beasts all bowed to me. Now, I am going to eat you!"

"I understand," said the monk. "But let me remove my tunic and robe. They won't taste very good."

Hongjun threw off his robe and tunic, exposing his red undergarments. Terrified of the color red, the nian monster ran to the back of its cave. "Go away! Go away! I can't bear to look at your red underwear!"

"No! I will not go away," said Hongjun sternly. "However, I will put my tunic and robe back on so you don't have to look at the red underclothes. But you must let me ride on your back."

"Okay! Okay! Just cover that red!"

Hongjun climbed on the tian monster's back and rode it into the town. "Dear people, you do not have to be afraid of the tian monster anymore," he announced. "He hates the color red, so just hang red banners and lanterns and paste red paper on your doors. The nian will not bother you."

The people followed Hongjun's advice, and that is why people wear red and cover their homes and streets with red lanterns and banners at the Chinese New Year. Hongjun also told them that the monster hated loud noise, so they set off firecrackers and created the lion dance to the deafening sound of drums and clanging cymbals.

Lion dance [68]

Another folktale explaining the origins of the Lantern Festival is the story of a girl named **Yuan Xiao**, which took place in the Han dynasty. Yuan Xiao, a young maid in the palace, was homesick for her family. As the Chinese New Year approached, Yuan Xiao grew increasingly depressed. The New Year celebration had always been a large family affair, with all the extended family—cousins, aunts, uncles—gathering at the ancestral village where her grandmother and grandfather lived.

"Now, I am all by myself. When will I ever see my family again?" Yuan Xiao wept as she sat next to a well, where she had come to draw water. "I want to jump into that well. What is the point of living without my family?"

She heard a man clearing his throat behind her. It was Dongfang Shuo, a palace official who had always been kind to her.

"Yuan Xiao, I am so sorry that you are missing your family at the new year." Dongfang Shuo said kindly. "I think I can help you reunite with your loved ones."

"Really?" Is that possible?" Yuan Xiao asked, wiping the tears from her cheeks.

"I have a plan. I think it will work. It's quite clever, really," Dongfang Shuo said, smiling.

The next day, another maid came running in to where Yuan Xiao was working. "Did you hear the news? Dongfang Shuo opened a fortune-telling booth in the market!"

"Dongfang Shuo? Telling the future? Does he have the gift?"

"Apparently," answered Yuan Xiao's co-worker. "He's saying that fire will destroy our city on the fifteenth day of the first lunar month."

"That's next week!" Yuan Xiao exclaimed. "I wonder what the emperor will do?"

The emperor had already called Dongfang Shuo in for a consultation. "How can I prevent this disaster?" he asked.

"The entire city needs to make offerings to the fire god," answered Dongfang Shuo. "Set off fireworks! Hang red lanterns and make yuanxiao (rice dumplings). Maybe the fire god will spare our city."

On the emperor's orders, everyone prepared for the festival. Yuan Xiao made the yuanxiao for everyone in the palace. That night, Dongfang Shuo led Yuan Xiao and other palace employees through the city filled with fireworks, red banners, and bright red lanterns. Crowds of people were enjoying the sights while eating rice dumplings. Suddenly, Yuan Xiao heard someone call her name.

"Yuan Xiao! Look, everyone. It's Yuan Xiao! Our daughter is here!"

Yuan Xiao peered through the smoke from the firecrackers. It was her family!

"Mama! Baba! Oh, and here's Granny and Grandpa! Sister! Brother! Oh, I have missed all of you so much!"

Yuan Xiao embraced her family. "Daughter," her father explained. "We came into the city to enjoy the celebration. It was a long way to travel, but we were also hoping to see you! Heaven has answered our prayers!"

Yuan Xiao turned to Dongfang Shuo. "Thank you, kind sir, for reuniting me with my family!"

At that moment, the emperor walked up. "Dongfang Shuo, this celebration has been a splendid success! I believe we have satisfied the fire god!" At that, the emperor winked at his minister. "Everyone is enjoying themselves, and families are reuniting. I decree that this festival of red lanterns and rice dumplings shall be an annual affair. We'll celebrate the fifteenth day after the first full moon of the year and name the festival after this young lady, Yuan Xiao! Her rice dumplings are the best I have ever eaten!"

The Moon Festival, also known as China's **Mid-Autumn Festival**, falls on the fifteenth day of the eighth month in the Chinese lunar calendar. In the Gregorian calendar, it is in late September or early October. One of China's oldest festivals, it is a harvest celebration that also celebrates the moon, which appears at its brightest this time of year. It is also a time to worship the moon goddess, Chang'e.

An image from the Luna spacecraft of the rabbit on the moon [69]

We learned in chapter two how Chang'e, the subject of many Chinese poems, got to the moon. She is sometimes called "Chang Xi," and one of China's oldest preserved texts, *Classics of Mountains and Seas*, writes of her bathing the moon. *Journey to the West* says Chang'e lived in "Guǎng Han Hong," or a cold, vast palace on the moon. Chang'e's pet, the Jade Rabbit, accompanied her to the moon. When the Chinese looked at the moon, they saw the image of the rabbit pounding herbs on a mortar for the immortals.

Journey to the West tells the story of how the Monkey King was fighting a demoness one day. Taiyin Xingjun, sometimes considered a manifestation of Chang'e, came down to Earth on a colored cloud. "Monkey King! The demon you are fighting is really my Jade Rabbit, she said. "She guards my palace on the moon, but she escaped, and it has been a year since I last saw her. Please spare her for my sake. I will take her back to the moon, and she will bother no one here on Earth."

The Monkey King reluctantly agreed, and Taiyin Xingjun took her rabbit back to the moon and gave it plenty of work to keep it busy.

At the Mid-Autumn Festival, the Chinese people celebrate the rice and wheat harvest by offering food and burning incense to the moon and praying to it. Families and friends gather outdoors to gaze at the moon, which symbolizes harmony. They eat mooncakes—dense, round pastries with a filling inside. Children have fun guessing what filling is in the mooncake. Is it sweet like lotus bean paste, or does it have a salted duck egg inside?

Dragon and lion dances are performed, and the ubiquitous red lanterns light the streets, symbolizing good fortune, happiness, and prosperity. One version of the story of Chang'e says that she and her husband were permitted to reunite once a year on the full moon of the eighth lunar month. The red lanterns lit the way for Chang'e on her journey back to her husband.

Conclusion

Chinese folktales open a window into Chinese culture and values. The themes and motifs presented in these chapters explore the interplay of history, mythology, and cultural identity. These tales of gods, heroes, magical creatures, and ordinary people impart moral lessons across generations. The stories reflect the deep-rooted philosophies that have permeated Chinese culture for thousands of years.

Several of these stories are macabre and brutal. Others are cloyingly sentimental. Some may be difficult to decipher from a Western mindset. Yet, together, they shed light on the soul of China, offering endless insights and inspiration. At first glance, some stories may seem simple, yet they convey deeper, symbolic morals. They explain how the world began, reinforce cultural traditions, and teach what is right and prudent through quintessential characters.

Many tales reflect Taoist, Buddhist, and Confucian values that still permeate China's culture. For instance, filial piety—the reverence, obedience, and concern for one's parents, older siblings, and elderly family members—shines through. Proper social hierarchy, especially within the family, is paramount in Chinese culture to this day.

Other religious and cultural values woven into these stories include Chinese concepts of immortality, balance, and integrity. The principle of yin and yang, representing opposing yet interrelated forces that embody balance and duality, serves as a foundational element in many Chinese folktales. Yin and yang are obvious in the primordial egg story yet quietly pervade the tale of the Herdsman and the Weaver Goddess—one from Earth and one from Heaven.

Several stories explore the pursuit of immortality through enlightenment and self-cultivation. Other tales teach moral values like honesty and humility. The story of Hui and the Golden Pheasant illustrates that dreams really can come true and that good intentions are worthy. The Monkey King tales emphasize that pride comes before a fall, yet tenacity and loyalty can save the day. Dashed hopes, realized dreams, magic, adventures, and cultural values—Chinese folktales have it all.

Here's another book by Enthralling History that you might like

Free limited time bonus

Stop for a moment. We have a free bonus set up for you. The problem is this: we forget 90% of everything that we read after 7 days. Crazy fact, right? Here's the solution: we've created a printable, 1-page pdf summary for this book that you're reading now. All you have to do to get your free pdf summary is to go to the following website:
https://livetolearn.lpages.co/enthrallinghistory/

Or, Scan the QR code!

Once you do, it will be intuitive. Enjoy, and thank you!

Further Reading and Reference

Part 1: History of China

Benjamin, G. Craig. The Big History of Civilizations.

Brewer, D. Quotes of Confucius and Their Interpretations: A Words of Wisdom Collection Book. 2020.

Brown, Kerry. XI: A Study in Power. 2022.

Clements, Jonathan. A Brief History of China. 2019.

Gernet, Jacques. A History of Chinese Civilization. 1972.

Gray, Henry John. China: A History of the Laws, Manners and Customs of the People. 1878.

Keay, John. China: A History. 2008.

Min, Anchee. China: People, Place, Culture, History. 2007.

Pletcher, Kenneth. The History of China. 2010.

Stuart-Fox, Martin. A Short History of China and Southeast Asia: Tribute, Trade, and Influence. 2003.

Tanner, Harold. China: A History From the Great Qing Empire through the People's Republic of China, 1644-2009. 2010.

Zedong, Mao. Quotations from Chairman Mao Tse-Tung (The Little Red Book). Pg. 1964.

Part 2: Chinese Folktales and Legends

Cutter, Robert Joe. The Poetry of Cao Zhi. De Gruyter, 2021.

Fu, Shelley, and Patrick Yee. Chinese Myths and Legends: The Monkey King and Other Adventures. Tuttle Publishing, 2018.

Hamilton, Mae. "Chinese God Pangu." Mythopedia. Accessed July 17, 2025. https://mythopedia.com/topics/pangu/.

Hamilton, Mae. "Chinese Goddess Nuwa." Mythopedia. Accessed July 17, 2025. https://mythopedia.com/topics/nuwa/.

Huang, Dehai. Illustrated Myths & Legends of China: The Ages of Chaos and Heroes. Shanghai Press, 2018.

Legge, James. The Notions of the Chinese Concerning Gods and Spirits. Hong Kong Register, 1852.

Ling, Vivian, Peng Wang, and Yang Xi. A Bilingual Treasury of Chinese Folktales: Ten Traditional Stories in Chinese and English. Tuttle Publishing, 2022.

Ling, Vivian, Peng Wang, and Yang Xi. Chinese Stories for Language Learners: A Treasury of Proverbs and Folktales in Chinese and English. Tuttle Publishing, 2019.

Macgowan, J. Chinese Folklore Tales. Macmillan and Co., Limited, 1910. https://www.worldoftales.com/Chinese_folktales.html#gsc.tab=0.

Nunes, Shiho S., and Lak-Khee Tay-Audouard. Chinese Folktales: The Dragon Slayer and Other Timeless Tales. Tuttle Publishing, 2021.

Personal Salvation and Filial Piety: Two Precious Scroll Narratives of Guanyin and Her Acolytes. Translated by Wilt L. Idema. University of Hawaii Press, 2008.

Pitman, Norman Hinsdale. A Chinese Wonder Book. E. P. Dutton & Co., 1919. https://www.worldoftales.com/Chinese_folktales.html#gsc.tab=0.

Selection from the Lotus Sutra: "The Daughter of the Dragon King." Asia for Educators: Columbia University, 1999. Accessed August 2, 2025. https://afe.easia.columbia.edu/ps/cup/lotus_sutra_dragon_king.pdf.

Sima Qian, Shiji, Records of the Grand Scribe. China Knowledge: An Encyclopaedia on Chinese History and Literature, 2010. Accessed March 13, 2025. http://www.chinaknowledge.de/Literature/Historiography/shiji.html.

The Ballad of Mulan: A Rhyming Translation. Translated by Evan Mantyk. The Society of Classical Poets, 2020. Accessed September 1, 2025. https://classicalpoets.org/2018/09/the-ballad-of-mulan-a-rhyming-translation/.

The Works of Motze. Confucius Publications, 1980.

Wilhelm, R., Norman Hinsdale Pitman, and Andrew Lang, eds. Chinese Fairy Tales, Folktales and Fables. Accessed July 15, 2025. https://fairytalez.com/region/chinese/#google_vignette.

Wu, Cheng'en. Monkey: Journey to the West. Translated by Arthur Waley. Penguin Classics, 1994.

Wu, Qinglong, Zhijun Zhao, Li Liu, et al. "Outburst Flood at 1920 BCE Supports Historicity of China's successful Flood and the Xia Dynasty." Science 353, no. 6299 (2016): 10.1126/science.aaf084 https://www.science.org/doi/10.1126/science.aaf0842.

"Yellow Emperor." China Daily.com. March 12, 2012. Accessed July 17, 2025. https://www.chinadaily.com.cn/life/yellow_emperor_memorial_ceremony/2012-03/12/content_14812971.htm.

Image Sources

1. SSYoung, CC BY-SA 4.0 <https://creativecommons.org/licenses/by-sa/4.0>, via Wikimedia Commons, https://commons.wikimedia.org/wiki/File:Teeth_of_Yuanmou_Man_(Cast)_-_cropped.png
2. Siyuwj, CC BY-SA 4.0 <https://creativecommons.org/licenses/by-sa/4.0>, via Wikimedia Commons, https://commons.wikimedia.org/wiki/File:Distant_dialogue_exhibition_of_Dadiwan_site,_2017-03-04_05.jpg
3. Daderot, CC0, via Wikimedia Commons, https://commons.wikimedia.org/wiki/File:Turquoise-Inlaid_Plaque_with_Stylized_Animal-Mask_Decoration,_1900-1350_BC,_Neolithic_to_Shang_period,_Erlitou_culture,_China,_bronze_with_turquoise_inlay_-_Sackler_Museum_-_DSC02627.JPG
4. Mlogic, CC BY-SA 3.0 <https://creativecommons.org/licenses/by-sa/3.0>, via Wikimedia Commons, https://commons.wikimedia.org/wiki/File:HouMuWuDingFullView.jpg
5. Territories_of_Dynasties_in_China.gif: Ian Kiu, CC BY-SA 3.0 <http://creativecommons.org/licenses/by-sa/3.0/>, via Wikimedia Commons, https://commons.wikimedia.org/wiki/File:Zhou_dynasty_1000_BC.png
6. Philg88, CC BY-SA 3.0 <https://creativecommons.org/licenses/by-sa/3.0>, via Wikimedia Commons, https://commons.wikimedia.org/wiki/File:EN-WarringStatesAll260BCE.jpg
7. SY, CC BY-SA 4.0 <https://creativecommons.org/licenses/by-sa/4.0>, via Wikimedia Commons, https://commons.wikimedia.org/wiki/File:Han_Expansion.png

8. Ian Kiu, CC BY-SA 3.0 <https://creativecommons.org/licenses/by-sa/3.0>, via Wikimedia Commons, https://commons.wikimedia.org/wiki/File:Western_Jeun_Dynasty_280_CE.png
9. Charlie fong, CC BY-SA 4.0 <https://creativecommons.org/licenses/by-sa/4.0>, via Wikimedia Commons, https://commons.wikimedia.org/wiki/File:Hangingtemple20190929.jpg
10. Yug, CC BY-SA 3.0 <https://creativecommons.org/licenses/by-sa/3.0>, via Wikimedia Commons, https://commons.wikimedia.org/wiki/File:China,_742.svg
11. SS, CC BY-SA 4.0 <https://creativecommons.org/licenses/by-sa/4.0>, via Wikimedia Commons, https://commons.wikimedia.org/wiki/File:Later_Han.png
12. https://commons.wikimedia.org/wiki/File:Leifeng_Pagoda_in_the_Southern_Song_Dynasty_by_Li_Song.jpg
13. Cattette, CC BY 4.0 <https://creativecommons.org/licenses/by/4.0>, via Wikimedia Commons, https://commons.wikimedia.org/wiki/File:Yuan_Dynasty_revised.png
14. https://commons.wikimedia.org/wiki/File:A_Seated_Portrait_of_Ming_Emperor_Taizu.jpg
15. Philg88: Attribution Wikimedia Foundation, www.wikimedia.org, CC BY 4.0 <https://creativecommons.org/licenses/by/4.0>, via Wikimedia Commons, https://commons.wikimedia.org/wiki/File:Qing_Empire_circa_1820_EN.svg
16. shizhao, CC BY-SA 2.0 <https://creativecommons.org/licenses/by-sa/2.0>, via Wikimedia Commons, https://commons.wikimedia.org/wiki/File:%E9%A2%90%E5%92%8C%E5%9B%AD%E4%B8%87%E5%AF%BF%E5%B1%B1%E4%BD%9B%E9%A6%99%E9%98%81.jpg
17. https://commons.wikimedia.org/wiki/File:Regaining_the_Provincial_Capital_of_Ruizhou.jpg
18. https://commons.wikimedia.org/wiki/File:Sunyatsen1.jpg
19. https://commons.wikimedia.org/wiki/File:Yuan_Shikai2.jpg
20. https://commons.wikimedia.org/wiki/File:Chinese_captives_in_Nanking.jpg
21. https://commons.wikimedia.org/wiki/File:President_Richard_Nixon_and_Mao_Zedong.jpg
22. 周流劲火, CC BY 2.5 <https://creativecommons.org/licenses/by/2.5>, via Wikimedia Commons, https://commons.wikimedia.org/wiki/File:Xiamen_Shimao_Straits_Tower_at_dusk.jpg
23. Officia do Palácio do Planalto, CC BY 2.0 <https://creativecommons.org/licenses/by/2.0>, via Wikimedia Commons, https://commons.wikimedia.org/wiki/File:Xi_Jinping_2019.jpg
24. RootOfAllLight, CC BY-SA 4.0 <https://creativecommons.org/licenses/by-sa/4.0>, via Wikimedia Commons: https://commons.wikimedia.org/wiki/File:Qilin.svg
25. https://commons.wikimedia.org/wiki/File:Anonymous-Fuxi_and_N%C3%BCwa.jpg

26 Gary Todd, CC0, via Wikimedia Commons: https://commons.wikimedia.org/wiki/File:Huangdi_Temple_-_Statue_of_Huangdi,_the_%22Yellow_Emperor%22.jpg

27 https://commons.wikimedia.org/wiki/File:Court_ladies_pounding_silk_from_a_painting_(%E6%8D%A3%E7%BB%83%E5%9B%BE)_by_Emperor_Huizong.jpg

28 https://commons.wikimedia.org/wiki/File:%E7%8E%89%E7%9A%87%E5%A4%A7%E5%B8%9D%E7%95%AB%E5%83%8F.jpg

29 https://commons.wikimedia.org/wiki/File:Chang%27e_flees_to_the_moon_by_Tsukioka_Yoshitoshi.jpg

30 ScribblingGeek, CC BY-SA 4.0 <https://creativecommons.org/licenses/by-sa/4.0>, via Wikimedia Commons: https://commons.wikimedia.org/wiki/File:Zhao_Gongming_Caishen.jpg

31 Rolf Müller (User:Rolfmueller), CC BY-SA 3.0 <http://creativecommons.org/licenses/by-sa/3.0/>, via Wikimedia Commons: https://commons.wikimedia.org/wiki/File:Fourheavenlykings4096x1360.jpg

32 https://commons.wikimedia.org/wiki/File:1962-01_1962%E5%B9%B4_%E6%B5%99%E6%B1%9F%E7%BB%8D%E5%89%A7_%E5%AD%99%E6%82%9F%E7%A9%BA.jpg

33 en:User:Wikiality123, CC BY-SA 3.0 <http://creativecommons.org/licenses/by-sa/3.0/>, via Wikimedia Commons; https://commons.wikimedia.org/wiki/File:Silk_Route_extant.JPG

34 VK Cheong, CC BY-SA 3.0 <https://creativecommons.org/licenses/by-sa/3.0>, via Wikimedia Commons: https://commons.wikimedia.org/wiki/File:Tang_-_Ferghana_War_Horse.JPG

35 https://commons.wikimedia.org/wiki/File:Flag_of_China_(1889%E2%80%931912).svg

36 https://commons.wikimedia.org/wiki/File:Xuanzang_w.jpg

37 https://commons.wikimedia.org/wiki/File:Eleven-Headed_Guanyin_(1943.57.14).jpg

38 https://commons.wikimedia.org/wiki/File:JourneytotheWest.jpg#file

39 Daftation, CC BY-SA 4.0 <https://creativecommons.org/licenses/by-sa/4.0>, via Wikimedia Commons: https://commons.wikimedia.org/wiki/File:Sacred_Lotus_in_a_Pond_2.jpg

40 https://commons.wikimedia.org/wiki/File:Eight_Immortals_Crossing_the_Sea_-_Project_Gutenberg_eText_15250.jpg

41 https://commons.wikimedia.org/wiki/File:Album_of_18_Daoist_Paintings_-_10.jpg

42 Collectie Wereldmuseum (v/h Tropenmuseum), part of the National Museum of World Cultures, CC BY-SA 3.0 <https://creativecommons.org/licenses/by-sa/3.0>, via Wikimedia Commons: https://commons.wikimedia.org/wiki/File:COLLECTIE_TROPENMUSEUM_Zilveren_Manjusri_beeld_afkomstig_uit_Ngemplak_Semongan_TMnr_10016132.jpg

43 Photo Dharma from Sadao, Thailand, CC BY 2.0 <https://creativecommons.org/licenses/by/2.0>, via Wikimedia Commons: https://commons.wikimedia.org/wiki/File:011_Long_Nu_(9212414191).jpg

44 atgu, CC BY-SA 3.0 <https://creativecommons.org/licenses/by-sa/3.0/>, via Wikimedia Commons: https://commons.wikimedia.org/wiki/File:Brand_-_panoramio.jpg

45 Mary Harrsch from Springfield, Oregon, USA, CC BY 2.0 <https://creativecommons.org/licenses/by/2.0>, via Wikimedia Commons: https://commons.wikimedia.org/wiki/File:Detail_from_plaque_depicting_the_Dragon_Boat_Festival_Cloisonne_enamel_1735-1795_Qing_dynasty_China_(3)_(253364827).jpg

46 Metropolitan Museum of Art, CC0, via Wikimedia Commons: https://commons.wikimedia.org/wiki/File:MET_TR.457.2012_image0002_(Moving_Chinese_dragon).jpg

47 Metropolitan Museum of Art, CC0, via Wikimedia Commons: https://commons.wikimedia.org/wiki/File:MET_30_75_5_d1.jpeg

48 User:Vmenkov, CC BY-SA 3.0 <http://creativecommons.org/licenses/by-sa/3.0/>, via Wikimedia Commons: https://commons.wikimedia.org/wiki/File:Hokkien-Huay-Kuan-2330.jpg

49 Isidijeron, CC BY-SA 4.0 <https://creativecommons.org/licenses/by-sa/4.0>, via Wikimedia Commons: https://commons.wikimedia.org/wiki/File:Nezha_contra_Ao_Guang.jpg

50 d'n'c from Beijing, CC BY-SA 2.0 <https://creativecommons.org/licenses/by-sa/2.0>, via Wikimedia Commons: https://commons.wikimedia.org/wiki/File:Sun_Wukong_at_Beijing_opera_-_Journey_to_the_West.jpg

51 https://commons.wikimedia.org/wiki/File:Ke_Jiusi-Twin_Bamboo.jpg

52 https://commons.wikimedia.org/wiki/File:Birds,_bamboo,_and_camelias_-_Google_Art_Project.jpg

53 https://commons.wikimedia.org/wiki/File:Dog_by_bamboo.jpg

54 User:Vmenkov, CC BY-SA 3.0 <https://creativecommons.org/licenses/by-sa/3.0>, via Wikimedia Commons: https://commons.wikimedia.org/wiki/File:Xiao_Xiu_-_NE_turtle_-_P1070560.JPG

55 https://commons.wikimedia.org/wiki/File:Yu_Sheng_-_Fenghuang_-_18th-century.jpg

56 https://commons.wikimedia.org/wiki/File:Twelve_Symbols_national_emblem_of_China.svg

57 Anonyme, CC0, via Wikimedia Commons: https://commons.wikimedia.org/wiki/File:Ph%C3%A9nix_ou_Fong_Hoang_pos%C3%A9_sur_un_rocher,_J_873(5).jpg

58 https://commons.wikimedia.org/wiki/File:Three_Brothers_edit.jpg#file

59 姜明雄, CC0, via Wikimedia Commons: https://commons.wikimedia.org/wiki/File:DSC07682_(30723853208).jpg

60 Morio, CC BY-SA 4.0 <https://creativecommons.org/licenses/by-sa/4.0>, via Wikimedia Commons: https://commons.wikimedia.org/wiki/File:Yue_Fei_statue_(Zhonglieci)_5_2016_January.jpg

61 https://commons.wikimedia.org/wiki/File:Yanju%27s_tomb,_nine-tailed_fox.jpg

62 Jakub Hałun, CC BY-SA 3.0 <https://creativecommons.org/licenses/by-sa/3.0>, via Wikimedia Commons: https://commons.wikimedia.org/wiki/File:20090524_Hangzhou_7423.jpg

63 https://commons.wikimedia.org/wiki/File:La_expedici%C3%B3n_de_Xu_Fu,_por_Utagawa_Kuniyoshi.jpg

64 Luca Casartelli, CC BY-SA 2.0 <https://creativecommons.org/licenses/by-sa/2.0>, via Wikimedia Commons: https://commons.wikimedia.org/wiki/File:Great_Wall_of_China_in_Beijing_(21006986438).jpg

65 Wang Hui (王翙), CC BY-SA 4.0 <https://creativecommons.org/licenses/by-sa/4.0>, via Wikimedia Commons: https://commons.wikimedia.org/wiki/File:E_Huang_and_N%C3%BC_Ying.jpg

66 Cleveland Museum of Art, CC0, via Wikimedia Commons: https://commons.wikimedia.org/wiki/File:Unknown_artist_-_Rank_Badge_with_Single_Crane_Motif_-_2019.78.1_-_Cleveland_Museum_of_Art.jpg

67 Silentpilot, CC0, via Wikimedia Commons: https://commons.wikimedia.org/wiki/File:Red-lantern-1202514.jpg

68 https://commons.wikimedia.org/wiki/File:Lion_dance2015.jpg

69 Zeimusu assumed (based on copyright claims)., CC BY-SA 3.0 <http://creativecommons.org/licenses/by-sa/3.0/>, via Wikimedia Commons: https://commons.wikimedia.org/wiki/File:Rabbit_in_the_moon_standing_by_pot.png

www.ingramcontent.com/pod-product-compliance
Lightning Source LLC
Chambersburg PA
CBHW050334010526
44119CB00004B/143